Scorpio

The Ultimate Guide to an Amazing Zodiac Sign in Astrology

© Copyright 2020

The content contained within this book may not be reproduced, duplicated or transmitted without direct written permission from the author or the publisher.

Under no circumstances will any blame or legal responsibility be held against the publisher, or author, for any damages, reparation, or monetary loss due to the information contained within this book, either directly or indirectly.

Legal Notice:

This book is copyright protected. It is only for personal use. You cannot amend, distribute, sell, use, quote or paraphrase any part, or the content within this book, without the consent of the author or publisher.

Disclaimer Notice:

Please note the information contained within this document is for educational and entertainment purposes only. All effort has been executed to present accurate, up to date, reliable, complete information. No warranties of any kind are declared or implied. Readers acknowledge that the author is not engaging in the rendering of legal, financial, medical or professional advice. The content within this book has been derived from various sources. Please consult a licensed professional before attempting any techniques outlined in this book.

By reading this document, the reader agrees that under no circumstances is the author responsible for any losses, direct or indirect, that are incurred as a result of the use of information contained within this document, including - but not limited to - errors, omissions, or inaccuracies.

Contents

INTRODUCTION 1
CHAPTER ONE: AN INTRODUCTION TO THE SCORPIO 4
    SUN SIGNS AND THEIR DIVISIONS 5
    THE SCORPIO (OCTOBER 23 – NOVEMBER 21) 8
    FAMOUS SCORPIOS 10
    THE SCORPIO AT WORK 10
    THE SCORPIO AT A PARTY 11
    THE SCORPIO AT HOME 12
CHAPTER TWO: SCORPIO STRENGTHS AND WEAKNESSES 14
    THE SCORPIO'S STRENGTHS 14
    THE SCORPIO'S WEAKNESSES AND HOW TO NAVIGATE THEM 17
    WHO YOU REALLY ARE 19
    WHO OTHERS SEE YOU AS 20
    THE SCORPIO IN THE FAMILY 20
    WATER MEETS EARTH 22
    WATER MEETS FIRE 22
    WATER MEETS AIR 22
    WATER MEETS WATER 23
    THE FIXED SCORPIO IN THE FAMILY 23
CHAPTER THREE: THE SCORPIO CHILD 25
    THE MALE SCORPIO CHILD 28

- THE FEMALE SCORPIO CHILD 29
- SCORPIO CHILD HEALTH 31
- HOBBIES OF SCORPIO KIDS 32
- THE SCORPIO CHILD AT SCHOOL 33
- PARENTING YOUR SCORPIO 33

CHAPTER FOUR: SCORPIO AND LOVE 35
- THE SCORPIO: LOVE SO DEEP 35
- CREATIVE IN LOVE 36
- THE JEALOUS SCORPIO 36
- THE DEPENDABLE SCORPIO 37
- BEST MATCHES 37
- WORST MATCHES 39
- THE SCORPIO WITH OTHER SIGNS 41
- THE TEEN SCORPIO AND RELATIONSHIPS 43
- THINKING LONG-TERM WITH THE SCORPIO 44
- QUICK FACTS ABOUT SCORPIOS 44
- OBSTACLES THAT ARISE WHEN DATING A SCORPIO 46
- QUICK GUIDE TO DATING A SCORPIO 46
- ATTRACTING THE SCORPIO WOMAN 48
- ATTRACTING THE SCORPIO MAN 49

CHAPTER FIVE: THE SOCIAL SCORPIO 51
- WHY THE SCORPIO IS AN AMAZING FRIEND 51
- WHY TRIBES MATTER TO SCORPIOS 53
- JOINING THE SCORPIO'S TRIBE 53
- THE FIRST RULE OF THE SCORPIO'S TRIBE: DON'T TALK ABOUT THE TRIBE 54
- THE SCORPIO'S HIGH SOCIAL IQ 55
- THE MOST SOCIALLY ENGAGED SIGN 56
- SCORPIO FRIENDSHIP COMPATIBILITY 57

CHAPTER SIX: SHADES OF SCORPIO 62
- DECANS 62
- THE THREE DECANS OF SCORPIO 63
- CUSPS 66
- SCORPIO CUSPS 67

CHAPTER SEVEN: THE PROFESSIONAL SCORPIO 70
    SCORPIO JOBS 71
    THE SCORPIO EMPLOYEE 74
    THE SCORPIO BOSS 76
    OBSTACLES THE SCORPIO FACES AT WORK 78

CHAPTER EIGHT: SCORPIO SEXUAL COMPATIBILITY 81
    THE SCORPIO AND FIDELITY 82

CHAPTER NINE: THE MOON SIGN 86
    THE SCORPIO MOON 87
    THE STILLEST AND DEEPEST OF WATERS 88
    CELEBRITIES WITH THEIR MOON IN SCORPIO 90

CHAPTER TEN: SCORPIO RISING 91
    ALL ABOUT RISING SIGNS 91
    FINDING YOUR RISING SIGN 92
    SCORPIO RISING 92

CONCLUSION 98

HERE'S ANOTHER BOOK BY MARI SILVA THAT YOU MIGHT LIKE 99

REFERENCES 100

Introduction

Astrology is important, and it's amazing how much insight you can find about your life from studying the way the stars affect your day-to-day choices. It has helped many people figure out why they act the way they do and what to do about it. I should know — I've enjoyed the benefit of understanding astrology for most of my life.

With astrology, you can finally get to know and understand the people around you - not just yourself. It is vital to have this level of understanding about life, allowing us to be more compassionate, loving, and accepting of the people around us at their best and at their worst. The second you become aware of where you stand among the stars, you can no longer go back to how you used to be. It's radically life-changing!

Within the field of astrology, you'll find so many terms that, while poetic, serve to flesh out every bit of the unique individual you are. You get to discover things about yourself you never even noticed about the one person you thought you knew the most: YOU!

In this book, you will discover what it means to be a Scorpio. You'll learn about your strengths, your weaknesses, and how you can take charge and overcome them so that you can be the best Scorpio you can. It might seem weird to most people to think of their lives as patterned after the stars, but the fact is that you are made of star-stuff! The essence of you is the essence of the cosmos. You're a walking, talking, breathing universe all on your own!

You see, astrology goes way beyond just putting all 7 billion-plus people on the planet into 12 boxes and calling it a day. It's so much more than that. Through astrology, you can learn how every single individual has unique needs, while at the same time being almost like everyone else. In other words, astrology can help you discover how we're all different *and the same.*

Since the beginning of time, humans have looked to the stars for wisdom and guidance in their affairs. So, you could say that the practice of astrology is as old as humans. Don't let its age fool you into thinking it is a field of study that is static – or dying because of unchanging ideologies. Often seen in Vedic, Chinese and even Western astrology, this continues evolve and provide new and profound insight as the years go by.

This book is all about the Scorpio zodiac sign of Western astrology. There are many levels to this sign, and as needed, we will veer off into discussing other zodiac signs as they tie in with the Scorpio.

That you're reading this says you're very interested in learning about the mysterious, magnetic Scorpio, because you are one yourself or you have a Scorpio in your life that you'd love to understand better. Well, you're in luck! With this book, you have all you need to know about this wonderful sun sign. Have fun peeling back the Scorpio's many layers!

One last thing: Astrology does not imply in any way, shape, or form that your life is locked in, predestined to be one way, and no way else. It doesn't suggest you are fated or doomed to live out your life on one track, never veering left or right. What astrology is about is helping you discover your strengths and weaknesses, so you can become a much better version of who you are. I'll wrap up this intro with the wise words of Sir Francis Bacon: "The stars do not compel; they impel."

Chapter One: An Introduction to the Scorpio

More often than not, when you hear someone say, "She's a Scorpio," they're talking about the Sun sign. The Sun sign is basically whatever point the Sun is at as it makes its way around the Earth each year, moving through all 12 signs of the zodiac.

In astrology, the Sun is a planet within its own right. It's the most powerful one, and for a good reason: All horoscopes have the Sun as the most influential star when it comes to how you live your life and how people see you. It influences your choices, your motivations, and your reasons for striving to achieve whatever desires you've set for yourself.

The Sun sign gives you the blueprint of who you are as an individual. It's the very foundation of your personality. Everything else that's stacked upon it may make one Scorpio somewhat different from another, but in the end, it gives a dependable picture of who you are. So, if you're hoping to understand your Scorpio lover, or friend, or family member, then you're doing a great job by looking into their Sun sign.

Maybe you've studied Scorpio astrology in the past and thought, "Hold on now, that is so not true! I'm not like that!" Well, that's usually because the Sun sign only gives you the basic outline of who you are. To get the full picture, you must look at your Moon sign and other factors. If you looked at your birth chart, you might learn that while the Sun was in Scorpio when you were born, the Moon was somewhere else.

Every planet on your birth chart can be at a different sign than others. This is precisely why you feel misunderstood when you read those horoscopes. It's the reason you're so unique and intricately complex. If all Scorpios in the world were the same, life wouldn't be near as fun!

To have a much more accurate picture of yourself, you must consider your birth chart in its entirety. Even after that, you must allow for the fact that you're human. You're very capable of breaking the mold that your Scorpio zodiac sign has assigned you if you want to.

While the stars may guide you, at the end of the day, you determine what you become. You're in charge, always! With that out of the way, know what your tendencies are as a Scorpio so you can have a better relationship with yourself. If you're not a Scorpio and just looking to understand this sign, you will find yourself better able to relate with them.

Sun Signs and Their Divisions

It is vital that we consider the ways in which the zodiac signs are grouped. So, let's get into it.

Dualities

As far as dualities go, every zodiac sign is feminine or masculine. There are six signs in each division. Each division is called duality. You might understand what it means to be feminine or masculine, but no matter what they are, neither is better than the other; they are simply neutral in respect to "better" or "worse."

Feminine signs are receptive, alluring, and magnetic. You'd think feminine signs are passive, weak, or bad, but that is not the case. Masculine signs are direct and energetic. Again, I must clarify that the masculine isn't better than the feminine or vice versa.

Think of feminine signs as possessing a vast ocean of quiet strength, being very self-constrained, and full of powerful inner resolve. But masculine signs portray strength by directing all-action outwards.

The feminine signs are Pisces, Taurus, Capricorn, Cancer, Virgo, and last but most definitely not least, Scorpio. The masculine signs are Gemini, Leo, Sagittarius, Libra, Aries, and Aquarius.

Triplicities

You can further classify each zodiac sign into groups of four. Since there are 12 signs, there will be three in each group. Therefore, they are called triplicities. Each triplicity is a representation of one of the four elements: Water, Earth, Fire, and Air. These are the elements that form the basic traits of the zodiac signs.

The Water signs — Scorpio, Cancer, and Pisces — are in tune with their emotions and their intuition. The Earth signs — Virgo, Capricorn, and Taurus — are some of the most practical and stable people you'll ever meet. The Fire signs — Leo, Sagittarius, and Aries — have a robust enthusiasm for life and are the most active signs. The Air signs — Aquarius, Libra, and Gemini — are very intellectual and adept communicators.

Quadruplicities

The 12 zodiac signs are also divided into three groups, with four signs per group. These groups are called quadruplicities. Each quadruplicity represents a specific quality:

- Fixed
- Mutable
- Cardinal

The fixed signs — Scorpio, Aquarius, Leo, and Taurus — are not particularly welcoming when it comes to change. That's actually a good thing, as it means they may not start things, but when they do, they set their minds squarely on the goal they need to accomplish and will not stop until they finish and perfect it.

The mutable signs — Virgo, Sagittarius, Pisces, and Gemini — are the most versatile of the lot. They can be flexible, and they're willing to bend and weave no matter what circumstances life throws at them. They're okay with adapting as needed.

The cardinal signs - Aries, Cancer, Capricorn, and Libra — are often the outgoing ones. They're very enterprising and love to start things.

Realize that no two zodiac signs are precisely the same combo of dualities, triplicities, quadruplicities, elements, and qualities. Each zodiac sign is unique and expresses itself in different ways from others.

Polarities

There are six polarities with two zodiac signs per group. The polarities consist of signs considered opposite to each other in terms of their traits and characteristics. Let's see what they are:

- Aquarius have grand hopes and ideals, while Leo is all about expressing their unique creativity and creating their own fun.
- Cancer is passionate about home life, while Capricorn cares about their public life.
- Aries is fully about self, while Libra focuses on creating partnerships.
- Gemini longs for self-expression, while Sagittarius is about processing higher thought and philosophy.
- Virgo is passionate about work and self-improvement, while Pisces is dreamy and self-delusional.

- Taurus prizes their personal possessions, while Scorpio is all about sharing their possessions and building grand legacies.

Every zodiac sign has special numbers and days, unique plants and colors, metals, places, jewels, and so on. Each sign also has good traits and challenges. Regarding colors, you need not live your life only wearing colors native to your sign. You can wear colors that aren't tied to the Scorpio, and you can take meetings on other days besides your lucky one. The world will not end, as you've probably already noticed. Having said that, you might be pleasantly delighted if you tried to incorporate these things which you're about to learn in your life. Now we've got the basics about groupings out of the way; we can turn our attention fully on the Scorpio, a magnificent, mysterious, magnetic sign.

The Scorpio (October 23 — November 21)

Here's a quick guide on everything you need to know about what it means to be a Scorpio.

- Your duality is feminine
- Your triplicity is Water
- Your quadruplicity or quality is fixed. You are very passionate, very emotional, and just as imaginative. You have persistence in spades. Passionate and emotional as you are, you can be subtle. You also are pretty unyielding and obstinate, sometimes.
- Your ruling planet is Pluto. This is the ancient god of the dead and the netherworld. According to astrology, Pluto oversees regeneration, and directs the beginning and ending of all phases of life.
- Your symbol is the Scorpion. This creature is deadly and can poison all enemies with a single, fatal sting.
- Your glyph or written symbol depicts the Scorpion's stinger connected to a symbol for human reproductive organs

— the part of the body ruled by Scorpio. This symbol represented the phoenix in ancient times. The phoenix symbolizes regeneration and immortality. The curved lines and arrow in the Scorpio's glyph symbolize strong emotions grounded in practicality and directed at a higher consciousness.

• Your dominant key phrase is *I Desire*.

• Your polarity is Taurus. Scorpio is focused on legacies and inheritance. You feel the call of destiny and a sense of purpose. You are happiest when you share your life-force with others. The Taurus, on the other hand, is about owning and possessing. Those who are born under the Taurus sign have a desire to have, take, possess, and collect. They have a hard time letting go of anything that they deem theirs.

• The body parts ruled by Scorpio are the genitals. Scorpios are prone to infections of the urinary system and venereal diseases. Because of their rather volatile emotions, they are also prone to ill health – or plain exhaustion.

• Your lucky day is Tuesday.

• Your lucky numbers are 2 and 4.

• Your magical birthstone is Topaz. This stone brings calm and serenity to your mind and keeps you safe from illness and enemies. It also helps you release your innate occult powers.

• Your special colors are maroon, burgundy, and crimson. These colors signify a deep, burning passion.

• Your cities are Liverpool, Newcastle, Washington, D.C., and New Orleans.

• Your countries are Morocco, Norway, Tahiti, and Algeria.

• Your flowers are Rhododendron and Chrysanthemum.

• Your trees are bushy trees and Blackthorn.

- Your metal is Plutonium.
- Your animals are crustaceans and insects.
- Your challenge: As a Scorpio, you tend to make other people angry because of how jealous and secretive you can get sometimes. With a temper that stings, you can make others so angry they become violent.

Famous Scorpios

1. Sylvia Plath
2. Charles Manson
3. Whoopie Goldberg
4. Julia Roberts
5. Hilary Rodham Clinton
6. Calvin Cline
7. Pablo Picasso
8. Marie Curie

The Scorpio at Work

When it comes to working, you'd be hard-pressed to find anyone as passionate as the Scorpio — except maybe the Virgo. The Scorpio is generally very zealous no matter what they are working on at the time. As a Scorpio, you are motivated to give 110 percent because you have a deep fear of failure, you're very loyal, and you bring a unique perspective to whatever challenges need to be solved at work.

You're very charming and have a strong will. You're magnetic — but of course, you already know that. With a personality like yours, you pull in your coworkers. Ironically, you like to operate alone. You like to take the lead on projects, but you're also comfortable following someone else's lead — as long as "someone else" knows what they're doing and is clear on what they want you to do. You love to go after your goals with all you've got, but you'd rather be left alone while you do so.

While you may have a strong fear of failure, you're different from others in that where that fear might paralyze them, you use it as fuel to propel you relentlessly toward success — and succeed you do.

If you've got a Scorpio as one of your team members, you will find them an invaluable asset. They are strong team players, though they'd rather handle the parts of the project that require no one else but them to get done. This could be somewhat of a challenge, but it's one that the Scorpio can easily handle with a little compromise. They have only to allocate time to work on group tasks and their personal tasks.

The Scorpio at a Party

At first blush, you might presume the Scorpio is way above mixing with the rest of boring humanity at your party, but that's not the case. As a Scorpio, you're not exactly a social butterfly. Some Scorpios can flutter about and be the life of the party, but those aren't the typical ones, and those guys and gals probably have some Air element influence, anyway. Mostly, a Scorpio couldn't care less about social cues or the right way to act at a party. What does that even mean, "right way?"

You're not a fan of chit-chat and small talk about nothing. You're to the point and have no trouble saying whatever "politically incorrect" thing you want to. It almost sounds like you're antisocial, but that is not true! What you are is *socially selective.*

You see, the thing about Scorpios is that they love nothing more than to vibe with their own tribe. With their tribe, they can socialize without a care in the world, morphing from that reserved person at the party to a carefree social butterfly. There's a very interesting thing about that tribe: It might not have more than ten people in it, assuming it's even more than three to begin with.

So, if you want the Scorpio to have a good time at your party, you'd better be a part of the tribe or let them bring along their own tribe. Then you're sure to have a good time. Other than that, you will simply have to allow the Scorpio time to figure out what everyone's about before they let loose.

The Scorpio at Home

The Scorpio is a water sign, and this means they're very calm. They're also just as versatile and passionate about everything. While some people might think the Scorpio's propensity for mystery and drama isn't so great, it's actually a good thing! Also, we'd all do well to remember there is no one as profoundly devoted and loyal as the Scorpio is.

Now when it comes to Scorpio's home, you can rest assured that they've channeled this level of devotion to making it somewhere they always want to come back to at the end of the day. As a Scorpio, your home has a very personal touch, with your own very dynamic, functional, and stunning installations, and your added nuances.

As much as you enjoy socializing with your tribe, you crave balance. For this reason, you need a space you can retreat to so you can recharge and be by yourself, somewhere away from life's constant hustle and bustle. You'd rather live somewhere that's far from the noise of the city.

Because of your mysterious air, you love strong and dark tones that ooze opulence. You aren't exactly a fan of white or pastel shades. You'd rather have rich blue, noble black, elegant grays (the darker, the better) and powerful wine-red tones, which you can contrast with one another.

Your home is your sanctuary, furnished with only the best materials. You will settle for nothing less than the finest, and you love that air of understated elegance and luxury. So, opt for metal, marble, leather, and the rarest of woods. You also enjoy having all that luxury graced with a touch of coziness, functionality, and comfort.

Chapter Two: Scorpio Strengths and Weaknesses

In this chapter, we'll be focusing on the Scorpio's strengths and weaknesses, whether they're your colleague, friend, family, or lover. Let's get right into it!

The Scorpio's Strengths

One of the most lovable traits of the Scorpio is that of idealism. This zodiac sign is all about extremes. You've probably heard of people born under this sign as weak yet powerful; cold, yet passionate; clinging, yet independent. As a Scorpio, you're a beautiful bundle of contradictions! You have both sides of the spectrum of human nature within you.

You're never one to do things halfway. Others find it easy to depend on you to get the job done. If you make a promise, you will definitely stand by it, unlike a sign like the flaky Pisces, for instance.

You're emotional, very magnetic and alluring, and you're very forceful in situations that call for a show of strength. Speaking of strength, you draw yours from deep reserves within you as a water sign, and you pull through most things that would have others caving easily. With you, the water element is fixed; you're like a deep and bottomless well, or an iceberg, if you prefer. It may seem to those who do not know you well enough that you're quite difficult to approach and pretty impassive, but beneath the surface, you have so much passion turbulently roiling, invisible to all but whoever you'll get close enough to see.

You may seem calm on the surface, giving a smile as needed, but you're very persistent about whatever you set your heart on, and you're very strong-willed as well. That you're strong-willed doesn't mean you're not willing to bend and weave a little in terms of finding solutions. Whenever things don't go your way, you're not the kind to bow your head in defeat. You spring right back up to your feet and try something new, again. No one is as adept or agile at you for spotting trouble or obstacles and elegantly getting around it all. You don't just find a way; you find a score of ways to get your goal. It is this flexible nature of yours that allows you to remain in control.

Your mind is very philosophical, and you might have a keen interest in religion – as well as the occult. You have an uncanny way of knowing what's going to happen before it does. Somehow, you also understand what it means to be human more than others, and without being consciously taught, you know of the deepest secrets of life.

Water signs are psychic, but with you, Scorpio, you can dive even deeper into the psychic world, deeper than most others. Where others would chicken out and run away, you run eagerly into the rabbit hole, eager to explore more of what is your natural playground. It's no coincidence you're this way. The Scorpio is a sign that reigns supreme over birth, death, sex, and regeneration. These are all aspects of human life we must all confront and which we all know next to nothing about. Most Scorpios are incredible surgeons, scientists, doctors, and spiritual leaders.

You're not the kind who is willing to just be okay with what appears on the surface. You're a deep diver, willing, longing to go deep beneath the surface. It doesn't matter what it is you're doing. You could be learning how to make cosmetics, or learning to levitate, or reading something just for fun. Even then, you pierce way beyond the surface of things, to see that which others would miss. It's just how you are.

You're so flexible and adaptable that it's nothing for you to take your very formidable drive and zeal and channel all of it into new endeavors. You're not afraid to dive into completely new careers or projects that you've never had to deal with. When disaster strikes, you will marshal every resource at your command to make sure it all ends successfully. No one is as shrewd and practical as you are. You are a champion at setting immediate goals that are real and tangible and making them happen. Your single-mindedness and amazing concentration will often get you success.

With money, you're clever. You're a conservative spender. Amassing wealth is easy for you. With business, you are the sort who will first do things and then announce you've done them. Your opponents could never keep up with you because you're always light years ahead of them.

It's a sad situation that a lot of astrologers do not ever mention just how kind, loving, loyal, generous, and gentle a Scorpio is. A lot of idealists in life follow the highest and most noble principles – and they are Scorpios. These people have been a wonderful force for positive change in the world and continue to be that way.

As a Scorpio, no other sign feels things as intensely as you do. Emotion rules the day with you. Whether love, work, hobbies, relationships, or causes, you're very passionate about it all.

The Scorpio's Weaknesses and How to Navigate Them

It's a travesty that you're so misunderstood compared to the other signs. You usually have your own agenda, and no one besides whoever you reveal them to will know anything. You have so much brilliance, and there is so much depth to you.

You may seem very much at ease, but no matter how relaxed you seem, there's a lot going on in your head. You're always trying to work out what to do next and strategizing your life. The reason you're this way is you need to be in control. If you're ever not in control, you interpret that to be putting yourself in danger, psychically. There's nothing you hate more than the thought of being out of control or relinquishing control to forces outside of you. For you, control equals safety.

You can use this control so it works well for you, by bringing sanity back in times of chaos, or by helping others to make a dream of theirs come true by teaching them to control themselves, or setting up your workspace and home space so you can perform at your best.

When the Scorpio isn't evolved, they often try to manipulate and control other people and situations for their own gain or greed. With this Scorpio, the tug of war between light and dark in their psyche is very real and very turbulent.

As a Scorpio, you can and should use that same fervor whenever you have a goal and put it into relationships that feed all parties involved. Invest this energy in personal projects that mean a lot to you. If you're not mindful, you might expend energy, time, and resources on things and people that do not deserve you. When you do this, it's inevitable that your efforts are wasted, and upon realizing it's all been for nothing, you focus inwards as you wallow in a sea of regret and loathing; this can easily cause you to become destructive to yourself and others.

Being very emotional, you avoid giving of yourself to causes and other people who aren't worthy. This is great when it's all good emotions, but when negative, the resentment, jealousy, and vengefulness you can unleash upon the world are beyond legendary. The only thing just as legendary is your ability to endure, your drive, and energy. So, seek to find meaning in your life. You will be best served by finding your deepest calling and following that with reckless abandon.

In relationships, your best and worst traits show up in full strength, and this can make your relationships a bit complicated – perhaps more than "a bit." It may seem odd, but you're the kind who can be affectionate, kind, and yet unpredictable and violent. Even when you're the happiest, there's still the possibility that your mood will swing the other way with the force of a thousand waves.

While you're very loyal to those who you consider your tribe, you can also be possessive and jealous. For you, it's not okay that anyone you care about or love might feel something for someone else besides you. It's because of your all-or-nothing nature that you're this way. Here is a list of words you often wonder what use they could serve in language: Casual, restraint, and moderation. You love fully and live it fully. There is no in-between.

You're the kind of person who absolutely will never forget when someone has been good to you, and you will do your best to pay back doubly. On the flip side, you never forgive a wrong, and you are more than willing to wait years at a time to attack back with vengeance. If you're not a Scorpio and are simply trying to understand the people born under this sign, then know this: You'd better never cross them. If you do, you will have crafted yourself the worst enemy in the world, one so subtle and so deadly, willing to burrow in the sands of time to await the perfect opportunity to strike you down with relish... much like the actual scorpion in the desert.

The Scorpio is fiercely competitive, although you'd never guess it just by watching them. As a Scorpio, you will save every valuable piece of information you come across, and when the right opportunity comes around, you will use it as needed. If a rival shows a hint of weakness, you'll be there posed and ready to move in for the kill.

You can get very obsessive about your goals or whatever drives you, and this can make you difficult to reason with. You'd rather control and dominate anyone who will give you even an inch to do so. You get very suspicious, and you're slow to let people in or trust them with your heart. The good thing is when you do let them in, you love them, truly and deeply. Learn to be more open to the world. Forget what the news says; not everything and everyone is out to get you. Open up, and you'd be surprised at the wonder and the gift that is humanity.

Who You Really Are

Dear Scorpio, you are a person of incredible willpower, strength, and determination. Sure, you might do a good job of seeming calm and unflappable on the outside, but deep down, you are a raging sea of emotions, which you do a good job of keeping under wraps by focusing it into activities you deem useful.

You're a very high achiever. You just "get it" with no effort — thanks to your psychic abilities, which you have come to know and trust during your life. You listen to your gut as it tells you to strive for more and greater, and you will not let yourself slack on that front.

When you see an opportunity for greatness, you are the person who goes over it with a microscope and a fine-tooth comb before you jump right in. You're a warrior with a lot of energy to fight for all you believe in. Your one ongoing lesson is to continue to channel your energy toward positive goals and ideals. As you do this, you will become one of the greatest people in life, always winning all the time. Sure, sometimes, it feels like you're a warrior all by yourself. You feel too complex to be understood, and you don't have the words to express what you feel. In those times, it remains perpetually clear that what you know what you want, you want it badly, and you will not stop until you've made it happen.

Who Others See You As

Because of how incredibly secretive you can be, people are so desperate to discover what makes you tick. In a group, you're likely the wise one people turn to for answers because you have an uncanny way of knowing how the future will go. You have deep insight when it comes to why others do the things they do.

One thing people know about you is how sensual you are. It's not unusual for them to fantasize about you making love to them, maybe forever. Some see you as being too ambitious, too controlling, and very hungry for power, but even with all of that, they see you as someone they can trust because you never make a promise you don't intend to keep.

The Scorpio in the Family

With family, no one loves as hard or as deep as the Scorpio. In the family, if you need help with a project or a problem, or you just need solid advice, the Scorpio is the best person you could count on to be there for you. There is no length they will not go to for you to see you smile!

However, if you ever cross a Scorpio, they're fine with cutting you off, blood or no. They will take a moment to feel terrible about the fact that you messed things up so badly between you two, but only just a moment. The next minute, they will not hesitate to cut you off. You might as well be dead to them — figuratively and literally.

It might seem a little too over the top, but remember this is a sign with whom there is no such thing as a middle ground. They don't do half measures, ever. So, if you value your relationship with your Scorpio, then you'd better never betray them. If you do, you can expect that they will not let up until they've had their revenge or until you've shown that you're truly and deeply sorry and are committed to changing your ways.

The Scorpio often falls back on their emotions and instincts, and because of this, they're the one in the family who feels other people's pain the most. Your Scorpio sibling or parent or child will often just get you, without you having to over-explain how you feel or what you're thinking. They are completely sympathetic and will go above and beyond to make you happy. In fact, the Scorpio regularly will ignore her own needs to focus on everyone else's in the family — especially if she's a parent.

Being a water sign, your Scorpio very well knows what human nature is like, so if you ever try to hide something from them, just know that it's pointless. If you think you succeeded at hiding it, then know that they're only choosing to ignore it and let you off the hook until you're ready to come to clean yourself.

The Scorpio mom is amazing because she knows her kids inside out. She knows when there's something wrong. It's the same thing with the youngest Scorpio in the house; they're very adept at being able to discern when something is off when there's tension or trouble. Without being taught, they just know how to show a lot more affection and to be gentler when they notice a sibling or a parent isn't feeling so great.

If you need the best advice, an ear to whine to, or support, then you can count on the Scorpio. However, there's nothing more irritating to the Scorpio than when people aren't even aware that they have needed to or that they aren't happy. Since the Scorpio is very subtle in how they express their very intense emotions, it can take a fair bit to learn how to read your Scorpio and realize they're not okay with something. That being said, taking the time to read their subtle cues is well worth the investment. You'll learn that while they can be moody at the most unpredictable of times, they are also the most fun, loving, affectionate, and playful people you'll ever meet.

Water Meets Earth

Water and Earth are elements that go together naturally, offering mutual benefits to each other. If you're an Earth sign, you and your Scorpio will get along fabulously well. Others will often envy this bond between you.

The Scorpio can offer the emotional support that Earth signs need so they can comfortably share their feelings. As for the Earth sign, they have more than enough patience to deal with the Scorpio's moodiness and complex nature. They are of the Earth; and like the Earth, they will always be there.

Water Meets Fire

Put Water and Fire together, and what do you get? A lot of steam! The Scorpio is a passionate sign on its own, and people born under this sign are volatile, acting out erratically. The same thing goes for the Fire signs as well — but that's about where it ends with their similarities.

Fire is often left scratching her head for figuring out the mystery and enigma that is the Scorpio. The Scorpio might be exhausted by Fire signs because of their ultra-grand, larger-than-life aura.

Fire signs are great at giving the Scorpio a lift in their mood because of their playfulness, and they help the Scorpio be more confident about expressing their feelings. The Scorpio gives back to the fire signs by teaching them how to mellow out, be less selfish, and more empathetic.

Water Meets Air

Believe it or not, Water and Air are opposites - at least, astrologically. Where the Air signs are okay with being vocal and logical, Scorpio is more emotive and intuitive, so the connection between these two will require a lot of effort for it to work.

For example, a Scorpio parent may get very frustrated with constant chatter from their Gemini kid. Although, it is still possible for these family members to be of benefit and balance each other out. The Scorpio can learn how to live life without being so grounded in emotions from the Gemini. Meanwhile, the Scorpio can show the Air signs that there's nothing wrong with expressing their emotions, rather than trying to rationalize everything.

Water Meets Water

The thing about other water signs and the Scorpio is there is a LOT of emotion. Maybe even too much. Sure, the Scorpio can understand all the other water signs, and they can figure out what the other person needs without them saying a word, but these signs together are likely to have standoffs full of pouting and sulking when they don't see eye to eye. For instance, the Scorpio can easily become impatient with the Pisces because the latter can be a tad too insensitive, and a Cancer will have issues with how intense the Scorpio is and their unwillingness to communicate.

The Fixed Scorpio in the Family

Fixed signs are set on doing things the way they intend to, and they're also consistent. This can be a good thing in that you can count on the Scorpio. On the other hand, this could be bad because they can get really stubborn and refuse to listen to advice no matter how well it could serve them.

As a Scorpio, you're not a big fan of taking risks without knowing what you're getting into first. Your fear of failure keeps you from being reckless, and so you're often in the family to sound a note of caution when someone's about to fall for a scam or something.

You're incredibly patient, and you persevere no matter how bad things get, so often, you might find yourself being the one everyone at home relies on — unless there's another Scorpio or fixed sign in the house that the family can lean on too.

Your family recognizes the resilience, strength of character, and stamina you have, and so they know they can count on you to pull them through rough times, down to the very end. Your family knows that you're dependable, loyal, diligent, and dedicated. They trust you, and you give them lots of reasons. Because of you, the family has a sense of stability.

Chapter Three: The Scorpio Child

Scorpio children are just as fascinating as adults are. We're going to dive into what you need to know so you can raise your Scorpio child right. Let's get right to it!

The Scorpio child is secretive. As you no doubt know by now, Scorpios love their secrets. The little Scorpio is no exception, as they keep many things bottled up within themselves. There's nothing they want more than a lot of quiet, alone time, as well as privacy so they can be themselves.

You should not think for even one second you could ever hide anything from this bright and intuitive kid! Your Scorpio child is an incredible master of perception and knows the second something's off. More likely than not, he's the one who will figure out all the family secrets. You could try to discourage her from making you bare your soul, but there's very little power you wield when she sets her intense gaze upon you.

The Scorpio child is really, sensitive. Sure, your kid might seem very calm and at ease to the ordinary eye, but your little one has the wildest emotional roller coaster within him. It goes super-fast, has crazy twists, and turns — and you can bet the speed and twists are even more intense the more silent your child is, whether he's silent because he's giving the silent treatment or just super quiet.

As a parent, you have one job only: You need to get him to come out with whatever is bugging him when you feel there's something he's not okay with. It's important that you begin from a young age to encourage him to share his feelings. You see, Scorpio kiddos are just as extreme in their emotions as adults. They can go from the longest pout you've ever seen to the cutest, warmest smile in a matter of seconds.

For the Scorpio child, you must always reassure them. You'd be hard-pressed to find a stronger kid! When they are feeling intimidated, they will not admit that to you or anyone else. The Scorpio child is bold, brave, and ready to take on any challenge or unfamiliar situation. However, they are often full of insecurities and fear.

For this reason, you've simply got to reassure your Scorpio child. They need you to let them know that everything's really, truly, okay. Dishonesty doesn't work; just let them know despite whatever's going on, things will be all right. Give this kid lots of affection the way she wants it. You could hug her, hold her, or if she's a toddler, you could cuddle with her. Only do this until she is comfortable again and then release her.

Your Scorpio kid loves mystery and intrigue. Your Scorpio kid is just like the scorpion in the sense they love two things: Darkness and hiding. Your little one loves games like hiding and seek and any other game that means he gets to pull a vanishing act.

There's nothing the Scorpio child loves more than fantasy, magic, and mystery. They're probably the one kid you have whose love for Harry Potter runs super deep. If you're looking for something and can't find it, best believe the Scorpio will sniff it out for you. They love when things are hidden and need to be found. You've got a little Sherlock on your hands!

No other kid is as strong-willed as your Scorpio kid. From the day she's born, your Scorpio baby owns you and everyone around you with her eyes. They can be unnerving, seeming to pierce through your soul and strip you down to who you *really* are. She also has energy for days and days!

Your Scorpio child will take every chance she gets to test boundaries and challenge whatever rules you've set for her. Being fiercely competitive, you can rest assured she will not stop until she wins. It doesn't matter what your little Scorpio is doing at the moment; you can bet that she's the best at it and will beat everyone else hands down.

Whatever you do, you must be gentle but firm when disciplining your wee Scorpio. Don't ever assume, "Oh, they're a kid, they won't remember anything." They do! They have the most amazing memories. Add to that their high propensity for vengeance and vindictiveness, and you don't want to cross them — no matter how little they are! No one can cook up schemes for revenge like the little Scorpio. No one can hold a grudge as long as they can either.

Your Scorpio is pretty intense. But you already knew that, didn't you? The Scorpio child is intriguing, magnetic, you could say. Whether they want to, they always draw a following — which is funny because your little Scorpio is probably an introvert, being born under this sign.

With the people who matter the most to the Scorpio — family and close friends — they are the most loyal little ones ever. They will fight for you if they love you. However, with strangers, the Scorpio kid is not necessarily the most caring. At best, they can be indifferent to people they don't know. At worst, they can be impolite, and sometimes they even get cruel — especially if your Scorpio child gets even a hint of weakness from whoever it is. It is up to you to teach them how to be gentle with other people's feelings.

Your little Scorpio is possessive. She might not necessarily be okay with having to share snacks or toys with the other kids. It's just a

Scorpio thing, really, but there's nothing you need to worry about. She can grow out of it with loving guidance from you. You need only to praise her whenever you notice her sharing with her siblings or with her friends.

Another thing you want to do is to make sure you give your little Scorpio a lot of your time. You want to make sure you spend time with your Scorpio one on one and make sure you do that on a schedule. If you don't, she might start to feel jealous, and those intense feelings will sooner or later come bursting out and scaring everyone. You know what they say: Hell hath no fury than a Scorpio baby ignored? Something like that.

The Male Scorpio Child

There's nothing your Scorpio son loves better than to dominate at home. Your child is very strong. He's got good health in spades and can be a tad aggressive, so you'll need to tame that trait in him. Your job is to be there as a sterling example to the male Scorpio, teaching him to respect authority and how to have a healthy attitude about losing to someone else. If you will teach your Scorpio son this, then you've simply got to make sure you and your spouse continue to show him these values in different ways so your Scorpio son can grow up a good guy.

Because your Scorpio son is of Water, you must learn how to balance, showing him affection by giving him structure. When you don't do this, your Scorpio son will simply retreat deeper and deeper into his shell. On the flip side, when you give him with lots of love and lots of structure, your Scorpio son will come out of his shell and will be very eager to share his feelings and thoughts with you, frankly and honestly.

When your Scorpio son hits his teens, he becomes territorial. If he needs a moment to sort through his thoughts, he will retreat to his bedroom and do just that at some point; that is his sacred space. You do not want to go in there uninvited. Do not desecrate it by barging in;

respect your teenager's need for space. Think of it as the cave your young scorpion retreats into and decompresses from the sensory overload they've had to experience.

Like Scorpio daughters, your Scorpio son wants nothing more than the truth from you at every point. This also means he expects that if you make a promise, you keep it. If you ever have to break your word to your Scorpio, son, then you'd better have a very, very good reason. Otherwise, it's better to stick to it or be like your Scorpio son: Simply never make promises you do not intend to move heaven and earth to fulfill.

When your Scorpio son becomes a young man, you'll notice that he's attractive to many people. It's important that you prepare for this stage by teaching him the importance of taking responsibility for his sexual prowess. You've also got to teach him that his partners are not trophies for him to brag about having, but actual human beings with feelings he would do well to respect.

The Female Scorpio Child

Your Scorpio girl is full of drive, with her eyes squarely on the future. You'll notice that your daughter will have strong desires to take on a certain career when she's much older. So, it's your job as a parent of this amazing child to give her every tool she could want or need to make her dreams happen.

Yes, over time, there will be changes to that dream. She might decide she no longer wants to be a magician and would rather be a violinist. Whatever the case, her passion and determination for her goals remain just as fiery, and you should always nurture her dreams. Never try to insist that she focus on one thing. Give her room to discover herself.

You'll notice that your Scorpio daughter tends to be very private, and this can make it tough to communicate with her. Sometimes, you need to lay all your cards on the table because this is the only way to encourage her to allow you to get a peek into her stormy head. She's got a knack for hiding things; it's no coincidence that she loves to play, hide, and seek! Another great thing about your very private Scorpio daughter is that she is the absolute best at keeping your secrets. She loves it when you share them with her because that says to her you trust her. She will keep your secret until the end of time.

Chances are you've noticed your Scorpio daughter loves the night. Being a night owl, you've got to give her structure with her bedtime routine. Your Scorpio child loves the dark. With all her heart, he believes there is a lot of magic in the darkness. So, don't be weirded out if you go to check on her during the night and find her little eyes are wide open!

As your Scorpio daughter grows, her love for the dark becomes a need to explore life and ask lots of questions. Do not, by any stretch of the imagination, think these questions are your run-of-the-mill silly questions either. They'll be deep and insightful and could even cause you to do some soul searching yourself. Here's a helpful hint: If she asks you something you don't have the answer to, please don't make one up. Explain to her you don't have the answer, but you will discover and let her know. If you don't, you will have her mind spinning in constant circles, and she'll retreat until she has an answer that works.

Your Scorpio daughter is sensitive, even more than you think. It's not unlike her to hold on to things that have hurt her badly, all while doing her best not to let it show. You must do what you can to help her let go of those troubling, painful emotions, especially as she becomes a teenager.

You can expect that as your Scorpio daughter becomes a teenager and then a woman, she will have many people interested in dating her because she's so very mysterious and alluring. Seriously, her magnetism is so strong that even if you're the toughest of parents, you will have a hard time keeping them away from her. What you should do instead is to instruct your daughter she deserves the best in a partner and show her that it's important to respect the other person's feelings.

Scorpio Child Health

Your Scorpio child could never be accused of not having energy. Still, your Scorpio child may be susceptible to illness, which often comes at the most unexpected of times. You want to be very aware of your Scorpio's diet, making sure it's got all the nutrients they need to stay strong and healthy.

As your Scorpio child gets older, they become susceptible to issues affecting their reproductive organs. They can get cystitis, eruptions, venereal infections, and urinary tract diseases. So, as soon as it is reasonable, you want to teach them about the importance of being clean and staying safe.

Another thing you want to know: your Scorpio child could become ill because of these difficult emotions. As they grow older, this could mean falling ill because of them being too stressed out or overstimulated. It's important that you teach them such helpful practices as mindfulness meditation, so you can help them stay on top of their feelings and decompress as needed.

A Scorpio has calcium sulfate as its cell salt. This is the salt that helps with repairing damaged tissues and keeping infectious diseases at bay. It's incredibly helpful for keeping the mouth, nose, throat, esophagus, intestinal pathways, and reproductive organs functioning in tiptop condition. When your Scorpio is deficient in this sale, they become more susceptible to sinus infections and colds that never go away, infertility, and skin eruptions that refuse to heal.

You want to make sure your Scorpio gets foods rich in calcium sulfate, like radishes, cauliflower, figs, onions, black cherries, tomatoes, and coconut. It's also vital that they get food that's loaded with calcium, like yogurt, cottage cheese, and milk. A high protein diet would serve them immensely. You also want to make sure they get their fruits and veggies, and if they must have bread, make it whole grain. Fish (and seafood in general), almonds, green salads, lentils, beet, betties, bananas, citrus fruits, walnuts, and pineapples are great for them.

Whatever you do, do not give your Scorpio large meals. Whatever they have in the evening needs to be light. Give them spring water, not tap water. Being a Water sign, it's important that your Scorpio stays hydrated. Also, the fact that your Scorpio is of Water means it's easy for them to pick up other people's negative emotions. This causes them to become moody, brood a lot, and blow problems out of proportion in their minds. Inevitably, this leads to health problems. Again, mindfulness meditation will help your Scorpio here.

Hobbies of Scorpio Kids

You can put your Scorpio kid in a class for whatever will need them to be dedicated to and patient with whatever is being taught. While the Scorpio son is very interested in joining the military or becoming a private eye, the Scorpio daughter is amazing at sports.

Scorpio kids will often grow up to become journalists or doctors. They have a great intuition and often know where to go for the hottest scoop, or how to treat a peculiar case. When it comes to picking their university, please don't pressure them. Let your Scorpio's intuition guide them. Also, don't pressure them into a profession – not even medicine or journalism. There are other things that the Scorpio excels at, you know. This is a very creative sign, and they can excel as actors, writers, craftsmen, whatever! Just allow them to follow their passion.

The Scorpio Child at School

With school, your child may dominate others in his class. However, your Scorpio kid is a fast learner. They're very astute, intelligent, and have a great work ethic even at such a young age. It's important that your Scorpio child always has something interesting and useful to keep him occupied so that his energy is always productively used.

If your Scorpio kid doesn't like something, best believe she will not be interested in learning it, no matter what you do. You've got to let her decide what topics she's most interested in. Often, she'll pick things that will prove useful to her over time.

Parenting Your Scorpio

When your Scorpio child is among her peers, she's easy to pick out. She's the one who's busy brooding, her eyes soulful, her head filled with so many thoughts. What's really going on is that she's observing everything around her carefully. She has mastered the art of observation without seeming like she's observing. With group activities, she joins in with her closest friends, with whom she shares a bond of loyalty and trust.

You'll notice that your Scorpio daughter or son has powerful emotions. It's these emotions that they use to explore their world. Sometimes, they get so intense that other kids are simply overpowered by it all. Even you can be overwhelmed by them! What you need to do as a parent is to let your Scorpio experience their emotions fully. Let them know it's okay to talk about how they feel and let it out in a healthy way.

When your Scorpio kid has an outburst, it's only because he's been holding on to it for so long, doing his best not to let things get to him. It's because he's finally reached the end of his rope. So, whatever you do, please do not treat these outbursts as though they were nothing more than just temper tantrums. Your Scorpio kid genuinely needs your help. Help them understand why they feel as deeply as they do, whereas other kids are more happy-go-lucky.

You can help your Scorpio release her emotions by encouraging her to explore creative activities, like writing, painting, music, gardening, photography, or any other art form. The Scorpio child is ridiculously talented. You'll find you don't even need to give them any formal lessons to learn to play an instrument or mold something. They're just naturals, thanks to their Water element, which puts them in touch with their intuition and gives them a natural appreciation for art and working with their hands.

Encourage your Scorpio child's psychic abilities. Teach them to rely on their intuition, as they're naturally intuitive. You can play a game of telepathy with them. You or your child acts as the sender, and the other person acts as the receiver. Whoever is playing the sender needs to think of a number or color or shape (whatever you want, really) and visualize it as clearly as you can. The receiver needs to sit with their eyes shut and their mind empty and then say the first thing that pops into their mind. You'll be amazed at the results!

Chapter Four: Scorpio and Love

Of all the zodiac signs, Scorpio is the most mysterious and most profound. When they're in love, a Scorpio is very intense and very devoted. Like the Cher song goes, this sign is all or nothing!

I should point out that you, dear Scorpio, when you have someone in your sights; you can get a bit melodramatic because of the conflicting emotions and complexities that plague you.

It's okay that you're this way. You're a Water sign. This means you'll push the Air away, wear down the earth, and put out the fire. Does this mean love is a tragedy for you? A thousand times, no! When you do let go completely and trust someone else with your heart, there's only one way to describe that relationship: magical.

The Scorpio: Love so Deep

Because of the Water influence, you will often feel your love for your partner deeply. You can become introspective and are driven by your emotions. Since the primary emotion in your relationship is love, you will climb mountains for this lucky person.

Since your quadruplicity is fixed, this means that your love runs deep. When you decide you've found the person you want to spend the rest of your life with, you decide. There are no ifs, ands, or buts.

You're going to hang on. You will fight for your relationship. Giving up is not in your vocabulary.

When you fall in love, it is unmistakable. You can feel it in your soul. For reasons beyond your comprehension, you want to be with this person. Sometimes you have the wish to control them, but consider keeping that in check.

As a Scorpio, you want to feel it all. You want the hours and the lows, the love, and the pain. You love how you feel, and you want more and more. You're fine with totally losing yourself in love, seeking, and allowing yourself to be radically changed by it.

The reason you're so intensely passionate, possessive, protective, and downright loyal as a lover is because of your fixed quadruplicity and the element of Water.

Creative in Love

As a Scorpio, you're unusually creative, and this same love for creativity comes to play when you're in love with someone. You dedicate the same passion you use in learning a piano piece or crafting a hedge fund strategy to loving this person.

You literally invest yourself in loving your partner. You want to follow this feeling until you're old, gray, and gone. You often will write poetry or song lyrics about the passion you feel. As a Scorpio, you consider your partner to be fortunate to have a lover as devoted and true as you. Light or dark as it may be, you find catharsis in expressing everything you feel in art. Small wonder then that a lot of Scorpios create great works of art inspired by love!

The Jealous Scorpio

You feel everything deeply. So, as deep as your love is, it can be a terrifying thing when you become jealous. Your jealousy is just as boundless as your love is. This can be a terrible thing if left unchecked.

Your water-driven and fixed nature, which mean you express and feel jealousy just as deeply as you do love. When you're jealous, you can become downright vengeful. You become very unforgiving. Whatever happens next, only the man in the sky could save your lover or whoever from you.

Whenever you have been spurned by a lover, you feel it like deep inside your soul. It feels like death — and no, that's not you being dramatic. It truly feels that way. It's only natural too because you're not like the Fire signs, which can be optimistic in the wake of a broken heart, or like the Earth signs, which can still find a way to be stable when love has left them, or like the Air signs who can nearly rationalize their pain away. You're a Scorpio, through and through. That means you feel. You're emotional, and extremely so.

The Dependable Scorpio

Sure, being with a Scorpio can be a rollercoaster ride for navigating the highs and lows of their emotions, but one thing you can count on for sure is that they are loyal and committed to you and only you.

Scorpio is very dependable. They'll ride out the highs and lows with you. If you give them the same faithfulness and loyalty, they will up the ante. Remember, this is a sign that makes a point of repaying everyone generously. Give good; you get a lot of good. Give bad... Well, you have only yourself to blame for whatever happens next.

Best Matches

Now let's take a quick look at the signs that are most compatible with the amazing Scorpio.

Virgo

Scorpio and Virgo are literally a match made in heaven, as they are one of the best pairings ever as far as astrology is concerned. You, Scorpio, are a wild one. You're intense. But the Virgo is one of the more practical and stable signs, and this makes you both a wonderful pairing, Water and Earth, fixed and mutable.

You both care a lot about whoever you're with. Virgo's nurture other people's needs before their own, and they will often be hard on themselves, simply because they feel like they're not giving enough of themselves or doing enough for their partner.

As for you, Scorpio, you're very trustworthy. You consider trust to be very important, right up there with loyalty, if you're going to make your relationship work. When a Virgo worms her way into your heart, you're very happy to lavish your love on her with an intensity that might scare off other signs, but *not the Virgo.*

Just like you, the Virgo feels deeply. You might not be as obvious about your deep emotions, but they're there. You worry a lot about your softness and vulnerability being out there for the world to see, so you keep it all under wraps until a Virgo makes you her last bus stop and breaks down your walls.

There is so much compatibility between you two, intellectually, and in the bedroom. Virgo is very willing to let you take the lead, and with your need for the control, you're more than happy to. The Virgo finds your confidence super attractive, and you, in turn, love that he can be trusting enough to let you be in control and not challenge you.

In a funny twist, the Virgo's willingness to let you be in charge brings out your softer, gentler side. Since the Virgo is of earth, rock steady, and calming, they can influence you to relax and put you at ease. The result is that you both have a very stable relationship, not plagued by volatility. Another thing that helps is that you both love your me-time and respect it when the other person needs their space. You're both good with finances and never have to worry about the other person overspending.

Scorpio and Cancer

These two have a lot of similarities, the most obvious being they're both water signs. The best part is that even their differences complement each other. Cancer and Scorpio enjoy a lot of intensity with emotions, which binds them together.

Both signs love their privacy, value loyalty, and are very in touch with their intuition, which makes things beautiful in the bedroom. You both know what the other person wants.

Because of the nurturing qualities of the Cancer, your insecurities are put at ease. While Cancer is as emotional as you are, they have fewer hang-ups about expressing how they feel. This is a good thing for you since they can show you it's okay to let it out. Also, the fact that Cancer is flexible will make for a great relationship between you two, since as a Scorpio, you're not too big on making compromises.

Scorpio and Pisces

You're an excellent match. The Pisces is gentle and loyal, and that works great for you, Scorpio, since you're not so quick to trust. This match works well because as a Scorpio you want to lead, and a Pisces is happy to follow in your footsteps. They'll let you take the reins and adjust to accommodate whatever you need. Sex is also amazing and passionate for this same reason, and it sure does help that both signs are full of emotion.

The Fish and The Scorpion both have a tendency for very dramatic mood swings, switching from high to low and back. This is great because they understand that about each other. However, the intensity of the highs and lows can cause a fair bit of drama.

Worst Matches

Scorpio and Sagittarius

These two signs have a lot of qualities that contrast and will often lead to lots of conflicts. You, Scorpio, are private and mysterious. The Sagittarius, however, is very blunt and open. You may not be so quick to show your hand, but Sagittarius is okay with sharing her entire history with people she met only two seconds ago.

Where you tend to be deep and intense, the Sagittarius would rather keep things light and airy. You don't quite enjoy their tendency to not take things seriously.

The Sagittarius is a huge fan of debate, whereas the Scorpio is really not into being challenged. Add to the Sagittarius tending to be insensitive in their openness and bluntness, and it just makes a relationship between you two darn near impossible. You're emotional, and you hate it when people are insensitive.

The final nail in the coffin is that here you're very prudent about your money; the Sagittarius is very reckless and an impulsive spender. Other signs might think them generous or spontaneous, but you just consider them wasteful.

Scorpio and Gemini

Gemini doesn't hold a candle to Scorpio when it comes to emotional depth. They simply cannot relate, which is why it could never work. Add in the Gemini being a social butterfly at heart, while the Scorpio is not terribly social, and you've got a recipe for heartbreak. Plus, Geminis love to be around people. For you, Scorpio, who needs her space, this could be a nightmare.

Whenever there is conflict, the Gemini falls back on teasing you. Other signs may enjoy this, but you find it very irritating as a Scorpio. In the end, you both could never work because the Gemini considers you a wet blanket, while you find them the most superficial person ever.

Scorpio and Aquarius

The problem with the Aquarius as far as you're concerned is that they're a tad too distant and emotionally shallow. If you've ever been in a relationship with one, you may have had to constantly go into battle with them. Your emotional needs were always challenged by their constant intellectual analysis and rationalization.

Like the Sagittarius, the Aquarius can be blunt when making his points. Sometimes, he pushes this bluntness to the point of harshness, which means they will inevitably say something that you would never forgive or forget, being the Scorpio you are.

You do have some compatibility in the bedroom. You're both very open to trying new and adventurous things. Also, make-up sex between you is explosive. Like a drug, you keep coming back for more, even though you know sooner or later this relationship must end.

The Scorpio with Other Signs

Scorpio and Taurus

If anyone understands your jealousy, it's the Taurus. In fact, they're even flattered by it. What you both have in common is that you're thrifty, loyal, and very ambitious.

Where the Taurus can be relaxed and chill, you are a tad too intense for them. However, the one thing that makes you both incompatible is this: You're both super stubborn, and you have terrible tempers. You'll need to work on this if you want to have lasting love with each other.

Scorpio and Libra

In so many ways, you're both opposites. You're emotional, but Libra is very analytical. You have an intimate circle of friends and love deep connections, but the Libra loves to have a lot of light banter with many people. You're super intense, but the Libra keeps it casual. You can make this relationship work if you are both willing to compromise.

Scorpio and Aries

Oh, how you love the passionate Aries! You love their fire, but one thing keeps you both from working seamlessly: you can't quite get Aries to commit. This is not a problem if you're not interested in settling down. Because of your shared passions, you can both have mind-blowing sex.

Aries is a whimsical person, while you're very practical compared to them. There's only one way to make this work: You must not get too jealous when you see Aries doing their thing, and Aries must settle down and commit to you.

Scorpio and Leo

You both have very strong personalities. You both love control. You're both loyal, although Scorpio strongly doubts that Leo even knows the meaning of the word "loyal," and for a good reason: Leo is a born flirt. All that is flirting will only make the Scorpio jealous and stark raving mad.

However, there is an upside: You both are incredible in the bedroom together. The chemistry is unparalleled! But if you're looking for something more than a roll in the sheets, you'll notice you both have an issue with letting the other take control, especially with the Scorpion's wish to take charge in the face of Lion's pride.

Scorpio and Capricorn

You're both ambitious, diligent about what you do, and loyal. Capricorn is nowhere near as emotional as you are, Scorpio, but you can get them to be more romantic and emotional. You love that the Capricorn is dependable and down to earth, while the Capricorn can't get enough of your passion. It's not a bad match!

Scorpio and Scorpio

This relationship is amazing, since you feel like you've finally found a lover who gets you completely. You both love that you're emotional and loyal to each other. However, there can be struggle with this relationship because you are way too alike. You might also find that you're not so excited because mysterious as you both are on your own, together, there's no mystery. Add in the fact that you don't quite like the negative traits inherent in people born under the same sign as you, and, well, this might not last.

The Teen Scorpio and Relationships

The teen Scorpio in love has an active imagination and the same intense feelings common to all Scorpios. When any other teen falls for a Scorpio teen, the pull is simply powerful. It's super tempting to check your brain at the door as you walk into the teen Scorpio's world.

The teen Scorpio can be very affectionate, more so because they've probably not yet had any experiences to feel jaded about love. Since the relationship is new to them, the teen gives their all and holds nothing back. Intense is the only word to describe any relationship the Scorpio teen is in.

However, the Scorpio teen is very given to melodrama, drumming up crises where none exists. They strongly need to oversee everything and everyone around them, and exert their influence on whoever they're with. In other words, the Scorpio teen is willful, often to the point of being bossy in their relationships.

Remember that your Scorpio teen thinks about sex more than most, is intense, and super obsessive. Despite – or because of all this – the Scorpio remains very powerful and intriguing. Once the Scorpio teen has someone in their sights, their single-minded focus alone is enough to make other teens go weak in the knees. Your Scorpio teen might never say it aloud, but they enjoy having others under their control.

In a relationship with the Scorpio teen, it would be unwise of their better half to tag them on a social media post without their permission. They're not a big fan of public displays of affection. Just because they let you take that intimate picture doesn't mean they want you to post it for the whole world to see.

The partner of a Scorpio teen in a relationship would be wise to take time to win over the Scorpio. Let them reveal themselves to you when they're ready and the way they want to.

Thinking Long-term with the Scorpio

When you finally win over the Scorpio, you must do everything you can to never betray them. They have incredibly high standards and will not be so willing or able to forgive you or forget what you did.

If you're a Scorpio, then you treasure loyalty, trust, and love. You give these things freely to those who have shown you they are worthy of them. However, when your lover crosses you, you make a point of having them earn back your love, assuming you don't decide to just call it quits.

You're always to the point and very focused. You don't do half measures, and the same thing goes with relationships. So, when you're with someone, you're not with them in the meantime. You're with them for the long haul.

If you're in a relationship with a Scorpio, expect to enjoy more love than you've ever imagined possible. Also, the fact that they're the most amazing conversationalists and are articulate makes them absolutely alluring to you.

One likelihood you can have with a Scorpio is that they will do their best to figure you out on every level. Something about the Scorpio's eyes makes you feel you have nothing to hide, and you'd better not try either. When you choose to lay yourself bare before them, being honest about who you are, you will simply make them fall even deeper for you.

Quick Facts about Scorpios

- They're awesome at leading, inspiring, and encouraging others.
- You don't want to hinder their personal growth, or they will ruin you.

- They're not fans of people who are fake or superficial. They prefer deep connections with people who are driven and passionate.
- They do okay with long-distance relationships, staying deeply loyal no matter what.
- They are very particular about their words. They mean what they say and say what they mean.
- They are deathly afraid of being betrayed. Scorpio's find it particularly difficult to deal with betrayal at any stage in the relationship.
- They treasure honesty from those they care about.
- They love to be right — but this isn't a bad thing! They simply need self-assurance that they're on the right path.
- There's nothing they love more than being understood.
- They can be incredibly stubborn, just like the Taurus. Still, they can be open to doing things differently when coaxed the right way.
- Cross a Scorpio and get the full impact of their wrath.
- They never give up on projects that matter to them.
- The Scorpio is the multi-tasker extraordinaire.
- They're super resourceful and very driven.
- They can be incredibly loving and so peaceful, but can be filled with intense loathing and start World War III on the other end of the spectrum.
- They're tough to read, but they're well aware of their emotions.
- No one will have your back as a Scorpio does.
- They're super fun and very creative. It's never a dull moment with this sign!
- They love sentimental gifts from people who matter.

- Let them down once, and you might never get another shot.
- The Scorpio isn't a fan of quitters.
- Who loves to go to the most far-flung locations in the world for a vacation? This sign.
- They detest unfair judgments.
- Your Scorpio can be your partner, lover, or friend for life.

Obstacles that Arise when Dating a Scorpio

It isn't easy loving a Scorpio, but if you can work with these facts about them, you'll find it's totally worth it:

- They take a fair bit of time before they open up.
- They can get a little moody sometimes.
- They will need alone time, and that's okay.
- There's never a moment they're not ready and raring to go with sex. If you have a high sex drive, then this shouldn't be a problem for you.

Quick Guide to Dating a Scorpio

Dressing seductively will score you a lot of points. With lust, the Scorpio reigns supreme above other signs. Looking good is worth it, but of course, you need to do more than look good.

Before they say yes to a date with you, chances are they've gone all detective on your case. They'll do more than look you up on Google. They have ways and means to figure out what you're really about and see if they want to explore you more in person.

The Scorpio is slow about love. They aren't the sort to fall in love at first sight, and even if they do, they will take things slow and steady. They love it when seduction is subtle and are not fans of a direct, vulgar, or brutish advance. Just because they love sex does not mean they do not have standards and dignity... And just because they have standards and dignity doesn't mean they are not masters in the bedroom. That thing you heard about Scorpios? It's true.

Expect that the Scorpio will ask you lots of questions, allowing you to reveal yourself while being very adept at giving you only enough information to make you feel like you've got enough information. If you're lucky enough for them to pursue things further with you, you'll realize how little you know — and it will be such a delight to you!

Pick a spot for your date that seems to be secret, one that not everyone goes to or knows of is good for the Scorpio. Pay attention to them. Sincerely, share your passions with them. If you're going to see a movie, make sure it's one that has some mystery that needs to be unraveled — and make it a complex one.

It is imperative you show yourself to be confident — not by faking it, but by being okay in your own skin. You can be supportive of the Scorpio, but for goodness sake, don't be cloying with your sympathy, and don't be patronizing in your "support."

Pay attention to the Scorpio so you can give them the most thoughtful gifts they want, and they will appreciate that. Organize a getaway for you both; go somewhere; no one knows who you both are, and somewhere no one you both know can find you. They'll appreciate that.

Whatever you do, don't tell lies to the Scorpio, not even to impress them. They'll know it, or they'll find out one way or another, and then it's over between you two. The Scorpio loves a challenge and loves to be in control. You may indulge them, but do so without giving your power away; otherwise, you will lose their respect.

You must consider your motive for dating them. If you're thinking of using the Scorpio, then you'd better rethink it. Attempting to boss your Scorpio around is pointless. One way or another, the Scorpio will get their way. Don't bother trying to compete with them.

The last thing you want to do is to be so mired in your insecurity or self-pity around them. They won't stand for it. It's unattractive and is bound to push them away. Also, don't be too desperate and assume that you two are now an item when the Scorpio hasn't expressly said so or acknowledged the same thing.

You must be respectful of the Scorpio's need for privacy, and that means you should share nothing intimate about your relationship with your friends, whether in person or on social media. Again, never tag them in anything without asking them if it's okay.

Attracting the Scorpio Woman

To attract the Scorpio woman, realize that she loves to wield her sexual power, and so you mustn't come on to her too soon or too strong. She needs her space. You can allow for a touch here, a look there. This is not the time to be impulsive.

You must respect her. She needs to know you will not flake out on them when things get intense because she gives herself completely when she falls in love. So, you'd be better off with a slow build so she has time to know who you are. She's more about your actions, not your words. She values devotion over-sentimentality or just being "cute."

If you're just a braggart with nothing to offer when it comes to actual experiences, she can spot that from a mile away. She knows her strengths and knows her weaknesses just as well. You'd be wise to be very upfront about yours, without being overconfident or having a woe-is-me attitude.

You want to be the sort of person who watches her back, doesn't tease her when she's dealing with serious issues and shows respect for her innermost needs. The Scorpio woman is very pragmatic and all about taking action. They may have psychic abilities and be in touch with their intuition, but they're also aware of reality. They love it when their partner is productive and determined to make something of themselves.

Finally, you must be steady and consistent. The Scorpio woman is not looking for someone going to "hit it and quit it." She wants someone to be there for the long haul.

Attracting the Scorpio Man

He is full of secrets, and they will not come spilling out of him any time soon. You would be better off questioning him about things like what he's interested in and other safe subjects. Be very clear that you're not interested in invading his privacy, and he will come to respect you more. You can be sure that as you relate, he's feeling you out on a gut level.

The last thing you want to do is tell all on your first date. The Scorpio man is not a fan of someone who spills their guts way too early. If you notice you talk too much after a drink or two, maybe you should tone down the drinking.

There's nothing the Scorpio man loves more than someone who is in complete control of their life. To turn him off, show yourself to be the exact opposite. If you have no confidence in who you are, you might find the Scorpio man's every judging eyes to be intimidating and too much to bear. Hang in there, and when he warms up to you, you will find it was worth the discomfort.

With conversations, you can't go wrong talking about dark mysteries, hauntings, and weird things about the human psyche. He thrives and revels in that kind of talk.

Be mindful that it might be hard to tell what he feels about you at first blush. However, if he calls you and asks for another meeting, then you know he's serious. His attention, like his sign, is fixed — on you! If you treat him casually or like he doesn't matter, prepare for a nasty reaction. Remember that the Scorpio man doesn't trust easily, so it's possible for things to not work out for reasons best known to him and out of your control.

One thing about the Scorpio man is that his sensuality is unparalleled, but you'd never guess it because he keeps it under wraps, carefully hidden by his immense ability to control himself. Don't be fooled, though. His basic element is Water, which only means one thing: He is deeply emotional, and acts based on how he feels.

The Scorpio man loves to be subtly seduced, so give him just a bit here, a bit there, so you have him dreaming about what more there is to come. He is fine with drawing out the pleasure and stacking block after block of sexual tension before finally giving in. Also, he loves discretion when in public, as it gives a lot of time for the tension between you both to build. You want to make sure you can save him something for when it's just you two alone.

Chapter Five: The Social Scorpio

As a Scorpio, you're probably sick and tired of being called antisocial. Again, you are anything but antisocial; you're simply very selective of who you spend time with. The only way people can get to know this about you is if they become a part of your tribe — the only people who ever see the warm, witty, loving side of you when you're not self-conscious and you're carefree.

Why The Scorpio is an Amazing Friend

Scorpios connect deeply with their tribe. When you're a Scorpio, and you're with the people you connect with deeply, you can be very charismatic, charming, and engaging. You're the kind of person who engages others emotionally and makes them feel okay to share their feelings.

When dealing with people outside of the tribe, you're not bothered to pretend as you care about them. Even if they're your mother's nearest and dearest friend, you won't act all warm and cuddly if you don't feel like it; you don't see what the big deal is. You might be cordial, but that's about it.

You're not mean; you're simply selective because you love your tribe with a passion. Anyone who thinks you're mean has read you wrong. You're a Scorpio, which means you're very much about conserving your energy. You don't give it out to random strangers. You like to be mindful of where your time, passion, and interest goes. You're not a fan of random people or large crowds. When you're with your tribe, you can be the most adorable and lovable person on Earth!

As a Scorpio, you prefer deep, meaningful bonds with people. Inevitably, that means you will only be able to bond with a finite amount of people so you don't drain all of your energy. You're particular about who you spend time and swap ideas with, and you want to make sure that you don't waste any of it all on connections that are barely there or superficial. That might be okay with Aquarius since they don't discriminate and can share their emotions and affections all over the place, albeit thinly, but that doesn't work for you.

When you have the attention of a Scorpio, they're validating you. They salute who you are. It's a gift that you should treasure because it's very rare for them to give such lavish attention to anyone like that. It's not something they give all the time or a gesture that you can dismiss as lacking in substance. The Scorpio differs greatly from other signs in this regard.

Scorpio's are very shallow and often believe everything is about them. They reserve their attentiveness and emotions for a specific few. If you're one of these special people, you can rest assured you're getting the ultimate insight, kindness, charm and affection. They love to share with anyone who becomes a part of their tribe.

Because of how strong their love and devotion are, it's important that the Scorpio disregards anyone who isn't part of his tribe. He's not keen on socializing. She cares little for chatting. They don't care much for any social prompts they might get.

If you're not in the Scorpio's tribe, you must learn not to take it personally because odds are it has nothing to do with you. And no, they're not being cold or arrogant or playing games with you either. They're just very selective about who they spend time with because they need to be able to preserve and protect their energy since, for the most part, they will often give others energy at their very own expense. It's a matter of survival, not snobbery.

Why Tribes Matter to Scorpios

The Scorpio holds her tribe in high esteem because this is a sign that's all about intimacy, not just in romance but in every form. Sure, the Scorpio is a very individualistic person. You might even be tempted to tag them, loners, since they don't feel a need to socialize or partner up with someone all day every day like the Gemini, Libra, or Pisces. That said, they can hop out of the loner bus now and then and spend a lot of their time and space with best buds.

Here's a Curious Fact About the Scorpio: Give them a romantic partner that's a great match, and they'll be fine. That's their primary need. There, they have no need for a platonic tribe, but they can still have one and love them as deeply and fiercely as they love their partner. Go figure.

Joining the Scorpio's Tribe

First, you must prove yourself to be trustworthy. When it comes to friendship with a Scorpio, you cannot afford to make a promise and not keep it! You must show loyalty and show that you're willing and able to communicate emotionally with them. Having said all this, this alone doesn't get you into the tribe.

You see, the Scorpio lives by its instincts. The Scorpio, you know, places a lot of value on the cosmic and the intangible. Picking their tribe can involve a lot of factors totally out of your control, and you could even say out of *their* control as well.

For instance, do you have chemistry? If you don't, how do you create it? You can't. It either is there for you both or isn't. Do you both have the feeling that you've known each other a lot longer than you really have? Do you fall seamlessly into conversations or just plain communion together? Do you feel comfortable together even when no one's saying anything? Do you experience a sense of synchronicity between you two when you talk, or joke, sing, dance, or cook together? It doesn't end there, though.

Part of these intangibles is that soul level call and response between two people who instantly get each other, so when one of you needs the other around, they're there and meeting the exact need every time. Also, do you know what it means to speak without words? Maybe you do, but does that happen between you and the Scorpio? Are you able to tell just from intuition how they're feeling or what they're thinking? Are you comfortable sharing your emotions even more than society would consider okay or normal, and if so, does the Scorpio sense that you're the kind of person willing to take that risk?

Also, consider if you're the type of person who can create changes in the Scorpio's life or set off a chain of events that rocks them but in a good way. Is this you? Are you able to keep secrets and take whatever is told to you right down to the grave? It might sound dramatic to you, but not to the Scorpio. Do you solemnly vow to be there for the Scorpio, to nurture the friendship just like you would a relationship? Again, you might think this is over the top, but that's not the case. If you still think so, then the Scorpio definitely doesn't intend to be your cup of tea. At best, you'll be an acquaintance, but never part of the tribe.

The First Rule of the Scorpio's Tribe: Don't Talk About the Tribe

Okay, not to be so dramatic, but if you're not a part of the Scorpio's tribe, you won't even know that they have one to begin with. You might never know who their people are, let alone their names. You might wrongly assume that the Scorpio is without friends. It's possible to even for the Scorpio's own family to be completely unaware of the fact that they have a whole freaking tribe of their own.

Within just moments of meeting someone else, you can tell as a Scorpio whether you want this person to be a part of your tribe. This feeling should not be compared to the sexual desire you may have had for this person, even those who have shared your bed in the past may not be let into your clan.

So, who makes up the tribe? Usually, you have Water signs as friends, especially fellow scorpions. You may also have people born under the Eighth house, and those with very intense Pluto influences. However, your tribe really comes down to your personal needs, your birth chart, what you like, and the energies you have in spades versus those you lack. There's no telling what it is that will draw you to someone else, so it's possible that your tribe is made up of several other signs.

The Scorpio's High Social IQ

Sure, to the untrained eye, it might seem that you have no form of social aptitude when dealing with the public. However, you have a lot of traits that show you to be socially intelligent, more so than most, and more than you're often willing to let on.

As a clear instance, your very astute observation skills, sharp and intense stares, and your ability to probe deeply into the psyche of whoever you're with is beyond amazon. You know how to read moods excellently. You read faces and places with just as much ease.

Someone uninformed might dismiss the Scorpio as a sociopath, but even they cannot deny that when you flip the switch, you're magnetic, and you ooze charm. It's the whole reason everyone wants you, or wants to be you, or wants to be around you. Some Scorpios can turn their magnetism and charm off and on as needed. There are others who will draw a crowd no matter what they do, even though they would rather go unnoticed.

The Most Socially Engaged Sign

We've already discussed the Scorpio's tendency to become disengaged, but this doesn't mean you're socially detached. It really means that you're engaged *socially*. In other words, you connect with whatever environment you find yourself in so deeply and intensely that you need to take a moment to keep yourself in check. You feel the need to repress the feelings inside of you, so you do your best to look unphased by them. On the inside, though, your reactions are off the charts because you're so in tune with the moment! This is another sign of your very high social IQ as a Scorpio.

You've simply got to continue to sort through all the frustrations around, so you know what or who deserves the intensity of your reactions, whether it's the outsider, a wallflower or someone who doesn't fit the mold. Then, of course, there are times when you very well know beneath all the seeming normalcy of things, something's not quite right, and perhaps even dangerous.

When you're a sensitive Scorpio, you find that some places have you so reactive that you can't stand to be there — ditto for some people, too. You can't stand to be in the same room as they are... Unless it's a part of your plan to get revenge or something of the sort. While other signs are fine with socially playing nice or ignoring whoever they've labeled "enemy," you feel the negative emotion so strongly that if you didn't get out of there yesterday, you're going to explode (or implode.)

When you're one of the stronger Scorpios, you have no issues totally shutting down and raising walls against all incoming stimuli so that it's just you in your own world, much like the Scorpio child does, so well to where parents and teachers often wrongly assume their child is autistic. This strategy, however, takes a lot out of you because it requires truckloads of concentration.

To wrap this all up: The Scorpio's ability to remain socially reserved is because of a very impressive level of discipline, all in the attempt to stop yourself from giving in to the temptation to use your Scorpio traits for ill instead of for good. You're very wise to be socially reserved. As any Scorpio who demonstrates "social promiscuity" can tell you — especially if they are young — there's a tendency to give in to such ungraceful behavior like manipulation, backstabbing, cattiness and gossip. They do this a lot more than any other zodiac sign. So, let no one make you feel like crap for being deliberate about how you socialize!

Scorpio Friendship Compatibility

Scorpio and Taurus: The bull is your astrological opposite. Yet, you know you know that all your secrets are safe with them, and you value that. While the bull may care little about your feelings sometimes, you don't pay as much attention to their wish to be comfortable. Still, Taurus has an amazing sense of humor and helps you find laughter even in sad or annoying things. What you offer to the Taurus is your uncannily accurate intuition, which keeps them from making rave mistakes they'll regret, especially with matters of the heart.

Scorpio and Aries: With this friendship, occasionally there will be flying sparks. That's one of the reasons you enjoy the Aries. They're not afraid to argue with you, and you relish every chance you get for some good sparring. It doesn't matter how much your views differ with politics and religion; you love that the ram has some fire going on! It's quite nearly as bright and as hot as your zest for life. How to maintain this wonderful friendship is to remember that the Aries never holds grudges, or at least they rarely ever do. Whenever you and your friend argue, they likely would have forgotten about it half an hour later. So, don't hold grudges against them, no matter how tempted you are to do so.

Scorpio and Cancer: Well, it's only natural for you water signs to get along! You love that the Cancer is incredibly affectionate. You'll never tell them this, but you enjoy it when they make you your favorite meal or get you your favorite drink. As for the crab, they love how you're able to tell what they're feeling without them having to say a word. They love you would never ever tease them for feeling the way they do and that you respect how sensitive they are. You both enjoy the water and probably love water sports like boating and swimming. You also both enjoy all activities that require using your hands — stuff like baking, sculpting, gardening, and so on. At the end of the day, no matter how boring or mundane what you're doing is, as long as you're doing it together, you both have the time of your lives.

Scorpio and Gemini: Gemini is really upbeat, and this contrasts with your own personality. This is one reason you enjoy being in their company. You love how they're able to send your blues running for the hills, thanks to their youthful spirit and their constant optimism. They help you remember that you should look on the bright side, no matter what. However, you can sometimes have an issue with their non-stop chatter, and in the same vein, they don't enjoy it when you get all moody and silent as usual. Still, you both are very fascinated with life, and you love to figure out the unanswered questions together. You both enjoy the mystery! This binds you both together.

Scorpio and Leo: Another optimistic sign, Leo, boggles your mind with how they always passionately pursue reasons to remain upbeat. You love it, and it captivates you to no end. When you're with Leo, everything just seems brighter. You find it hilarious when they try to establish control over you, and you wonder how they could ever assume that they can get the upper hand as far as your friendship goes. The lion is innocent. You know this. They are too pure to beat a lifelong strategist like yourself. Still, occasionally you should stroke the lion's ego. It's only fair since they're supportive when it comes to your talents.

Scorpio and Libra: Oh, the Libra. So charming. So impossible to resist. You love how beautiful and graceful they are. You're a complete sucker for their wit. You're a lot more emotional than they are since they're very light-hearted. For this reason, you both can have misunderstandings now and then. You might think that their casual statement was them being caustically chastising you. You're not the kind to be vocal about your displeasures, and so when they say something that rubs you wrong, it's way too easy to ruin your friendship. Here's a tip for keeping this friendship going: If they say something or do something that gets to you, then you should speak up about it right away rather than sit and stew. After all, you can trust the scales to weigh and address your complaints in a balanced way.

Scorpio and Sagittarius: The Sagittarius loves to have fun. You? Not always. That said, you still have a lot to gain from this upbeat friend, while they could take a page or two from you by learning to be sober when needed. The archer is the person who helps you open your mind so that you're willing to meet new people, have new experiences, and come up with new, brilliant ideas. You get to show them how it can be dangerous not to be discerning and discriminatory when needed. This friendship works for you both in that regard. Now, you may not care for their bluntness, which is legendary, but admit that your penchant for keeping secrets drives the Sagittarius up the wall! Still, these are just minor issues to be concerned about when you're both doing things you love to do together.

Scorpio and Aquarius: No one is as unpredictable as Aquarius. As good as you are at reading people, this sign is a challenge. You can't find a single logical thing about the way they act — and oddly enough, this is why you are full of admiration for the water bearer. You love that they have the most unorthodox ideas. They keep you entertained. Sure, you might find that Aquarius is, well, all over the place with the things they're interested in. Still, you love how loyal they are. For you, their loyalty is all that counts. For Aquarius, they absolutely cannot resist your charms. Each day, they continue to be shocked at how well you can deduce things that lurk beneath the surface, unnoticed by others. If you're okay with how forgetful they are, then they can make peace with how jealous you get, and you can both be great pals.

Scorpio and Capricorn: You love how stable Capricorn is, and they love how passionate you are. When things get a bit too much for you, the goat will always be there with their stabilizing influence. They have the most practical advice, which you will find to be amazing. They'll keep you clear-headed and still, no matter how stormy things get. You are great at helping Capricorn find their inner spark whenever they become overwhelmed by the world and its issues. You may not like how pushy Capricorn gets, and they may not like that you're never willing to just let things go, but at your core, you both share the depth and a lot of similar interests.

Scorpio and Pisces: Your bond with Pisces is soul deep. This is one person who is okay with you and all your faults and warts. Chances are, they were drawn to you because of your faults, to begin with. They just love when people have flaws because, to them, it makes people more human and relatable, and this is why you guys have a good thing going on. They love spiritual issues, just like you do. Like you, they desire intellectual conversations about the law of attraction, religion or philosophy. You might be irritated by their tendency to hop from opinion to opinion, but this isn't a big deal because there's so much you love about hanging out with them. In any case, you're not perfect either. The fish is not a fan of your intense obsession over a love interest.

Scorpio and Virgo: There's not a better friend to have by your side than the Virgo. Because they're so down-to-earth, they will give you the perspective you need on anything. If you feel like you need someone to give you a reality check or tell you the truth without sugarcoating it, then the Virgo is your pal. When the Virgo analyzes whatever you share with them carefully, they'll let you know what they think is the most honest yet tactful way possible, respecting your feelings. Your Virgo friend is full of admiration for you, just as much as you love the gifts they share with you. The level of your intensity continues to be an inspiration to the Virgo, who's a tad shy about sharing how they feel. Thanks to you, they can learn to turn their love for writing, reading, or anything else into an actual passion. Now, the Virgo is prone to nitpicking, and this can irk you sometimes. But your habit of holding grudges will drive them nuts with impatience. After all is said and done, a little understanding from both of you will go a long way towards building a lifelong friendship.

Scorpio and Scorpio: When you're friends with another scorpion, it's an exquisite pleasure and exquisite pain! You love them because, finally, here's someone who understands your intense passion for life. As for the pain, it's because you're both experts at going down to the very depths of hopeless despair. Still, there's an upside to being friends with another Scorpio: You both have a deliciously dark sense of humor, which proves useful when things get tough for either or both of you. You'll get mad at each other and explode; there's no avoiding that when it's two scorpions in a friendship. Still, you'll wind up finding each other again and again because there's nothing more amazing than the empathy you both share, which creates an allure too intense to resist.

Chapter Six: Shades of Scorpio

Your sun sign is split into cusps and decanates, or decans, if you will. These are basically categories that help you further define yourself as the person you are, rather than just a simple focus on your sun sign all by itself. Everyone's birthday falls under a certain decan and cusp of their sign. We're going to look at each one in detail below.

Decans

All zodiac signs are split into three unique categories, with each called a *decan*. This term comes from the Greek word *dekanoi*, which translates to "separated by ten days." Originally, the Egyptians had this term. They had a calendar which assigned 360 days to a year. Another interesting thing about the Egyptian calendar was that each year had 12 months, each made up of thirty days — and that meant no one born on the 29th of February ever had to worry about celebrating every four years, which is a good thing. Now, each month of their calendar was split into three parts, with each part comprising ten days. These ten days were known as dekanoi.

To date, astrology still divides the zodiac into decans. Think of a circle that is 360 degrees as a whole; one decan would be no more than a 10-degree part of that circle, which lasts for just ten days before the next decan takes over. Each day, the sun goes through this zodiac circle by just one degree. Yes, this is not entirely accurate since we now work with a calendar where some months are over 30 days and one month has a day that ghosts us all every four years, but you get the idea.

I want to clarify that a sign's decan does not radically change the traits of that sign. It does improve the connection that the person has to their sign. If you're a Scorpio born in the fifth decan, you can expect to differ greatly from another Scorpio born in the second decan.

Each decan is assigned to a constellation. Every constellation has its own spiritual implications, which lend themselves further to making you unique. And each decan is ruled by a planet, often called a *sub ruler*. Think of the sub ruler like the second in command or vice president. It simply enhances your unique qualities within your decan.

The Three Decans of Scorpio

As you're a water sign, here are the three decans you need to know about as a Scorpio. You'll learn which one you are soon enough.

The First Decan – Intensity: October 23 and November 2

Being born under the first decan means you are Scorpio/Scorpio. Your ruling planets are Mars and Pluto. You're the purest of Scorpios, and your Scorpio energy is enhanced in good and bad ways.

You can remain calm even in the face of danger or the toughest of situations, thanks to Mars and Pluto, when they offer you strong support. However, when the planets are challenged, maybe you can have extreme fears. Still, it doesn't matter because you're always more than prepared for the worst.

You're the most sensual of the Scorpios, and your libido is unparalleled. You have obsessive tendencies, strong desires, and are beyond driven. As much as you love pleasure, you are also open to grief, loss, sorrow, and suffering. You don't think things come easy; still, you have a bulldog-like tenacity for getting what you want. You have the willpower and courage you need to overcome the odds, and you are amazing at rebounding when things don't work out, and at starting anew.

You're a loner for the most part, and you're very secretive about your personal business. You're not the kind who's super talkative or friendly at first blush. Your eyes can be rather intimidating to those not bold enough to meet fire with fire. You might also seem unapproachable or cold, or sometimes even cruel.

According to evolutionary astrologers, you're the one just learning how to make use of your energies as a Scorpio, and you might make a few mistakes you need to learn from during your life.

In tarot, the Scorpio's first decan is represented by the Five of Cups. The keywords of this decan are grief, loss, and anger.

The Second Decan – Transmutation: November 2 to November 11

You're a Scorpio/Pisces. Just as driven as any other Scorpio, but also possessing the Pisces energy and the rulers Jupiter and Neptune, all of which moderate your drive. The most common themes in the lives of those born under this decan are death and resurrection.

If this is you, you feel as though you have a much higher purpose than most. You'll go through a lot of transmutation in the process of figuring out what that purpose could be. When Jupiter and Neptune are properly placed in your chart, it's possible and easy for you to figure out your talents and gifts. If these planets aren't well placed, you might find you don't have as much faith in yourself as you should, and you don't trust others as much as you should, which could lead to you being needlessly scared of failing or being betrayed.

As a Scorpio/Pisces, you seek wisdom. You love it when you deal with smoke and mirrors, hidden meanings, and elusive hints. You crave mystery and are not afraid of taking a walk on the dark side. You care about the occult, the mystical, the esoteric. You are always looking for what is real and true, and as such, you will sacrifice whatever you must find it.

Your magnetism is beautifully raw. It never wavers, and it is extremely seductive. You might find yourself as a healer, always willing to sacrifice yourself. You might have a bit of a God complex, adept in the art of manipulation, unparalleled when it comes to your cunning, which you use to gain control over other people. Your mysterious aura draws people to you.

In the tarot, Scorpio's second decan is represented by the Six of Cups. Your keywords are peace, forgiveness, and harmony.

The Third Decan — Manifestation: November 12 to November 22

As a Scorpio/Cancer, your Scorpio energy is tempered by Cancer and the Moon. You have emotional integrity, and you're comfortable trusting your feelings. You're not the sort who would ever give in to compromise.

You tend to sacrifice yourself and take care of the people nearest and dearest to you, but you're also sensitive, and so you get hurt easily. You'll never show the pain openly, of course, but you never forget what caused it to begin with. When time and chance present themselves, you will exact revenge, and do so generously.

You have deep and dark emotions running through you as a Scorpio/Cancer. When the Moon is challenged on your chart, you could easily just bury everything you're feeling while feeling lonely, lost, and abandoned. When your Moon is properly placed, you are better at dealing with your painful emotions. It's easier for you to observe them, and as such, you can be forgiving of yourself and others and to be more accepting.

Your willpower is a Scorpio/Cancer is unparalleled, as is your self-confidence. You have it in you to always do good and sensitive. You can be a compelling writer or speaker who moves people forcefully thanks to your eloquence and compassion. Your charm also makes it, so you always get results when you work with a group, or you're going after something that you believe in heart and soul.

The Scorpio's third decan in the tarot is the Seven of Cups. Your keywords are finding where you fit in, soul searching, and self-examination.

Cusps

Now let's talk about cusps. If you've ever bothered to read material on various zodiac signs, chances are you've thought to yourself, "Well, why do I feel like Scorpio and Libra wrapped in one?" You wonder if there's any truth in astrology and you wonder if it's not just a bunch of people writing many things about people born in each month and hoping some of it sticks. Well, there's an explanation for that.

Every zodiac sign has something called a cusp, which is basically like the boundary between one sign and the next. Say your birthday is right when the sun is moving from one zodiac sign to the next; that would mean you were born on a cusp, and you would express yourself not as one sign but two! Sometimes both energies blend beautifully, while other times, it's a bumpy ride. Still, depending on the cusp you're born into, you take on certain qualities:

- Aries/Taurus — the power cusp: April 16 — 22
- Taurus/Gemini — the energy cusp: May 17 — 23
- Gemini/Cancer — the magic cusp: June 17 — 23
- Cancer/Leo — the oscillation cusp: July 19 — 25
- Leo/Virgo — the exposure cusp: August 19 — 25
- Virgo/Libra — the beauty cusp: September 19 — 25
- Libra/Scorpio — the drama cusp: October 19 — 25

- Scorpio/Sagittarius — the revolution cusp: November 18 – 24
- Sagittarius/Capricorn — the prophecy cusp: December 18 – 24
  - Capricorn/Aquarius — the mystery cusp: January 16 – 23
  - Aquarius/Pisces — the sensitivity cusp: February 15 – 21
  - Pisces/Aries — the rebirth cusp: March 17 – 23

Scorpio Cusps

The Drama Cusp, Libra/Scorpio: If this is your cusp, then you're ruled by Pluto and Venus. You're the type of person who is quick to let people know exactly what you're thinking, even if it will be painful to hear. It would be best if no one asks you a question that could lead to a hurtful, blistering truth unless they're ready for it. It's a great trait to have for work and at home, but if you are not mindful of how you drop your truth bombs, you might bruise a lot of heart.

You can be critical. You can be tenacious. And you can be oh so seductive. Because you're very willing and able to tell the truth, you have the upper hand when it comes to your social interactions with others. You're brimming with charisma because you have tons of sexual energy, pure and raw, and you're also charming in a very detached way. You can get sarcastic sometimes and even bossy, but in all of that, your honesty makes you the object of admiration.

With relationships as someone born on the cusp of Libra and Scorpio, you're super loyal and romantic. The problem is, your loyalty is so intense that you can get jealous sometimes, and that jealousy can wreck your love life if you don't watch it. Fortunately, you've got a very dogged tenacity about you, so if you want to do your best to keep your jealousy in check, you will find a way to do just that.

Your ability to stay determined and single-minded about your goals is great with work, as you often make your big goals happen. You can have a bit of ego, though, so you want to pause and think through things when you feel unwilling or unable to change something.

An important thing to do all the time is a check-in with yourself about your ego. You want to know if it's in the way of you becoming the best version of yourself. While you do this, you need to apply the same honesty you dish out to everyone to yourself as well and be just as brutal. Cut off anything you don't need that's getting in your way, whether it's a habit or a person who drains you every time you meet.

A final note for those born on the Libra-Scorpio cusp: Jealousy is something you want to quash. It will do nothing good for you. You want to learn to trust yourself and the people around you. Sure, you don't like the sound of this advice (or any advice, for that matter, since you'd rather people minded their own business and left you alone), but it will help you to take it in the long run.

The Revolution Cusp, Scorpio/Sagittarius: This is quite the combination, with the Scorpio, intense and dark, and the Sagittarius, active and bold. You're ruled by Mars, Pluto, and Jupiter. Your whole life is about going against conventions. If you learn that something should be done a certain way, you'll seek additional ways to do the same thing. You're the type of person who becomes an expert at anything easily, by teaching yourself. You love to learn by doing an activity and getting your hands dirty. Astrologers consider you to be the zodiac's wild child and a rebel at heart as a child.

When you do grow up, you can be contrarian, rebellious, and revolutionary. You're a true leader, with no fear whatsoever. You take everything you've ever learned during your many adventures and apply that towards becoming the best of authority figures. It's possible for you to become a truly powerful person, ever progressive, but here's the thing: You need to learn to always be objective and never let your emotions cloud your judgment. If you give in to knee-jerk reactions, that could be your undoing.

When you're born on this cusp and the Scorpio energy is stronger than the Sagittarius, you'll notice that jealousy is your weak point and could cause your possible downfall. You're possessive when you're in a relationship, but on the flip side, you're loving, romantic, and kind. You are competitive, often competing against yourself, allowing you to achieve great success. You have a drive that makes you see things through to the end, and never, not once, do you not complete something you set out to achieve.

Being a Scorpio/Sagittarius means you will be at loggerheads with authority, so ditch the thought of a 9 to 5 job and consider becoming your own boss. Chances are, you already know this, and you've already set things up, so you never have to answer to anyone that isn't you. If this is you, be mindful: Always be kind and generous with your professional life.

Something to remember as a Scorpio/Sagittarius is that you can get pessimistic, adopting a dreary, been-there-done-that frame of mind. For this reason, you tend to feel left out of things. However, you've got a lust for life unmatched by any other, and that makes you a super amazing person!

Chapter Seven: The Professional Scorpio

That people are very drawn to you, dear Scorpio, can be very useful in your career. You're one of the most ambitious and determined of workers, and you know without a shadow of a doubt what it is you want to achieve professionally.

You're determined to make your dreams come true, and you know just how to strategize your way to success. It also helps that you're able to keep a level head when everyone's losing theirs because of a chaotic event. You're more patient than most, and you can endure the highs and lows of whatever your professional life throws at you.

You're not a fan of taking orders, and you'd rather work on your own. You're the best at giving orders, though — quite literally. You'd do excellently well in the military. Despite this, you're not the type of person who likes to be in the limelight, professionally. For you, it's all about pulling strings behind the scenes because, as far as you're concerned, that is where true power lies. You could make a wonderful tax inspector, or a detective, police officer, or even a spy.

You have an innate ability to lead, heal, investigate, create, and touch people with your talent and your mind. That you're very curious about everything and you're passionate about the mystical things in life means you could also do well with pathology, psychology, and research.

Science is a field you should consider, as scorpions are great physicians, and usually the best of surgeons. You could also excel in art, journalism, and literature if you consider those professions.

You're the type of person who instinctively knows the difference between right and wrong, even when others can't really see it. Therefore, you will be excellent in the business, as long as you work independently and don't feel like you're confined. You are the woman with the words that flow like honey. It's not unusual for your presence to be requested at things like TED talks because you're a powerful orator, and you write as powerfully as well. Consider a career in marketing, or maybe even politics.

So, you have a rough idea of the kinds of jobs you can handle. Let's really get into a few that you just might find to be a perfect fit and why you should consider making a career change if you're not already doing something you would naturally find fulfilling.

Scorpio Jobs

As a Scorpio, you're magnificent in terms of jobs. You work hard, and your powers of perception are extraordinary. You love when your work has zero distractions, and don't be so accessible to everyone. You love it when you can do things the way you want to. However, here are some positions you should consider:

Detective: You're infinitely curious, and you love to discover secrets while holding on to your own. So, you'd be really good at figuring out all the stuff people do their best to keep under wraps. You're amazing at going undercover, silently watching everyone like a hawk while they remain blissfully unaware that they're giving themselves away. You're the best of researchers, and you never stop until you've uncovered everything. It also helps that you have a thing for revenge. You could also be a life coach, a private investigator, or a journalist.

Chemist: You love work that is scientific in nature. Through your curiosity, you'll be able to come up with new reactions or even challenge the status quo in your field. Your hands are steady, and your love for research will serve you well in this profession. For these reasons, you should also consider these professions: biologist, coroner, oncologist.

Pharmacist: You're very hardworking and ambitious, but more than that, you are the type of person who is enduring and has lots of fortitude. These traits make you very suited to being a pharmacist. Sure, there's a lot of education involved, and you've got to be as precise as possible, but you'd really shine here, combining your science know-how with your people skills all well-being left alone to do quality work. You could also be a surgeon.

Psychiatrist: Of course, this job has you all over it! You get to hear all sorts of salacious secrets — all while helping your clients to figure out the messes in their lives and feel better. You're amazing at mapping out the human psyche and looking closely at details, and this line of work will keep you very engaged. You'll also be immensely successful at it. Other professions like this for you to consider are therapist, guidance counselor, biographer, memoirist, anthropologist.

Surgeon: You're driven, intense, and have endurance in spades. You're also plagued by a need for excellence in all you do, and you always get said excellence. It's for this reason that you would do fabulously well as a Surgeon. Your tenacity and deep reserves of inner strength allow you to continue what you're doing, even when others have lost hope. Other professions you should consider are EMT, tradesperson, electrician.

Researcher: You can find a fair number of scorpions in scientific labs, deeply immersed in research for the government or private agencies. You love nothing more than to consider a problem and then figure out how to deal with it. You're great at evaluating conundrums and coming up with results. You need to be the best at everything that makes you more likely to be the researcher who comes up with the answer to eradicating the common cold and cancer or coming up with an amazing weight loss fix. Consider these other professions as well: marketing executive, consultant, analyst.

Auditor: Your keen eye for details, precision, tenacity, and endurance will ensure your success in this field. You have no issues sifting through all sorts of data for hours on end. You're very effective at communicating and just as dependable, which means you're the kind who can make critical decisions. Also consider these professions: data analyst, accountant, researcher.

Human Resources: You would have no problems going over the most convoluted of health plans and working out all 401ks. You're good at remaining on top of things when it comes to employee records, as well as figuring out their very complicated needs. You know how to manage several things at once, and you know how to prioritize effectively. You'd be amazing at this profession, but you could also consider these: systems engineer, cultural architect, chief operating officer.

Hypnotist: You love to be in control, and you're enamored with the human mind — the unconscious where all sorts of dark wonders lie in wait for you to discover. You can work with clients trying to break terrible habits or get over phobias. You'd have to suggest things to them while they're under hypnosis to help them with these issues or help them remember things they've buried and tucked away from their conscious mind, or even help them recall their past lives. You are the go-to sign for all things hidden and secret. Also consider these professions: astrologist, medium, psychic.

Sex Therapist: If anyone has issues in the bedroom that need fixing, you're the best person for the job. Imagine it: You get to hear all sorts of fascinating secrets, learn about people's sexual fantasies and all other embarrassing things people would rather not share — and none of that phases you. You're Scorpio, after all! Nothing could shock you, and you have a knack for getting right to the heart of the issue. You, better than anyone else, can help your clients to work through their bedroom problems. You should also consider these occupations: life coach, occupational therapist, urologist, OB-GYN.

The Scorpio Employee

You're highly determined to get things done. You're never confused about the things you want to achieve or the means you need to make them happen. You're the type of person who moves with a sense of purpose, remaining steadfast to your goals. When you've been assigned a task, your boss knows that it's already a done deal. You're going to make sure they get what they want, no matter what.

You've got a very analytical mind. You've got one of the most perceptive and sharpest minds of all the signs, while also being aware of your true nature. You are the employee who understands what other people are thinking and feeling without them having to say a word.

You know what drives your colleagues — or what would drive them to action if they're not moving as hard or as fast as you'd like. You know their weaknesses and their strengths, and you use this knowledge to get them to pull their own weight, whether it's about completing a task, demanding better pay, or anything else.

You're extremely confident in yourself and your abilities, for a good reason. The Taurus and Capricorn may know a thing or two about being determined, but something sets you besides these signs: You know darned well what you're good at, and you trust yourself implicitly to handle whatever needs to be done.

You're not the sort who deludes themselves, and you'd never lie to yourself about your weaknesses, strengths, and motivations. You've got this quiet self-assurance that has nothing to do with an ego like it would with Aries or with self-aggrandizement like it would with Leo. You're self-assured because you know yourself objectively. You're not the kind of employee who would blame other workers for what you know is your own fault. Instead, you set about fixing things and coming out on top!

You crave power. Usually, this motivates you. It's the reason you do all you do. It's not about needing to feel secure, like the Taurus, and it's not about wanting to put amazing ideas into action like the Aquarian employee. For you, you're about the power, which means your position, your influence over others, and all the trappings that come with being the head honcho or the one who moves and shakes things.

Your need for power will shape your relationships with your coworkers. You're the person who will try again and again, despite constantly being told "no." You are unflappable in the face of rejection because you believe that you will have your way sooner or later. You're not fazed by tantrums either, and you're happy to allow people to have their way because you know in your heart that you're the one who really is central to their success.

As a Scorpio employee, you know very well that the way to get power is through your boss, and so you will do everything your boss asks. If a coworker were to rub you the wrong way, they should watch their back. You are legendary when it comes to revenge and vindictiveness, using your fatal sting on all who you believe deserve it. You're not likely to forgive a wrong, no matter how much time has passed or how many times you've gotten an apology. When the time is right, that coworker will regret not leaving the company the day you took on the job.

It would be wise for your boss to treat you with dignity and caution, no matter how accommodating you are. You will find a way to match their position or surpass them. The last thing they need is to be on your bad side.

You are super secretive. You're reserved and cautious. You don't engage in social relationships at work because you love your privacy, and you don't think it's necessary. You'd rather have lunch on your own, not chat it up at the water cooler. You won't be caught dead trying to organize the Christmas party, that's for sure. If anyone wants to get along with you well at work, then it would be wise for them not to go poking and prodding about your social or personal life.

You are calm on the outside, yet you feel things intensely. With working, you only ever allow just a glimpse of your strong emotions to come through, often in a quick flash of anger or annoyance or in a warm look of appreciation. You're a pro at hiding how you feel, and your emotions will remain hidden.

In the end, you're an employee with your own business to run: Becoming number one. Your steely tenacity, sharp mind, and unswerving courage mean that wherever you work, you're that company's most valuable asset.

The Scorpio Boss

You're very determined. As a Scorpio boss, you're courageous and tenacious, and these are the qualities that have landed you where you are. You're not afraid to take risks, even in the face of insurmountable difficulties. You're going to start, and you're going to finish what you start. You're not the type of person who opts out of things you've gotten yourself into, no matter what happens. This is why you're the best at leading others, and you're the best at dealing with crises in the company.

Because of your courage and dogged determination, you expect others to give you the same energy. Never are you indecisive or squeamish about making tough decisions. You march on in confidence well-founded in your abilities. For you, it's not a popularity contest. You will put your employees through whatever you believe is necessary to get the best out of them.

You're extremely temperamental. You oscillate between extreme emotions. You're better at keeping your emotions in check at work than in love, but sometimes you show these emotions by being very critical of an employee who messed up while being full of praise moments later. You're not like the Libra, who maintains balance and poise. You're the type of boss who doesn't mind playing head games with your employees if you sincerely believe it will get them to do their best work.

You're cautious and hold on to your secrets. You're not like the Cancer or Libra boss who gets chatty with the employees about their family. You will never give them even an inkling about what you're thinking. There's no point in your employees trying to know your business because they'll get nothing out of you and will only annoy the heck out of you.

You seem very calm and collected, yet you are full of all sorts of very intense emotions. Your passion knows no bounds — and it's the whole reason you choose to be secretive to protect yourself from those who would exploit these emotions. You're never going to bare it all for everyone to see because you believe it would lead to disaster, hurt, and disappointment.

You're extremely perceptive. Your powers of perception are unparalleled, and they help you keep control of your employees. You're able to tell what people are all about with mind-boggling accuracy. You can get right to other people's core and understand what makes them tick. Therefore, you have a natural bent for the occult and the psychic, especially if you're female. Anyone who wants to impress you had better be honest about themselves, as with your eyes alone, you can cut through deception like a hot knife through butter — and you detest dishonesty deeply.

You're possessive and jealous. With the people you care about, you're *very* possessive. How does this translate to work? Well, your employee had better mind themselves when it comes to moonlighting or their allegiances to whoever you consider "the enemy," which could be a rival company or brand or someone else who is vying for their seat.

A Libran boss may be able to demonstrate equanimity, but no one should expect you, the Scorpio boss, to understand that the only reason you were just face-timing the head of a department in a rival company is that they're your brother's wife. Either the employee deals with you and your company alone, or they resign.

If an employee ever tries to put one over you, then they have better just clear their desk. You're the type of boss who will exact vengeance if you feel you've been betrayed or cheated, and there is no length you will not go to teach the offending employee a lesson.

It could be a tad daunting working for a boss like you, but your employees are thankful because they can borrow a leaf from your determination and drive as they observe you working. They need only to be honest, hardworking, and loyal, and they'll have a swell time at the office with you!

Obstacles the Scorpio Faces at Work

Your vindictiveness can be a problem. Because of your vindictive nature, you may run into some problems at work. This same vindictiveness could very well hold you back from true greatness. You really should learn to let go of grievances. You can't always have everything you want, and you need to make peace with that fact.

Also, you'll want to get a grip on the underlying aggression which hides beneath your calm and collected exterior because occasionally it could break out — and it could mean the difference between advancing in your career or remaining stuck where you are.

You're not a team player. If you work in a solitary environment, this is okay, but when you work with others, your ambition combined with your secretive nature is detrimental. You might consider your coworkers to be your competition and wall yourself off from them. You want to dial back your intensity and give cooperation a chance. You might like it! Or not. That's okay.

You must resist the urge to play dirty. Let's not sugarcoat this fact: No one's a better, more cunning, diabolical schemer than you are. You have dirty tricks that *have dirty tricks* for days up to your many, many sleeves. This is great when you're on the battlefield, and you're a general going up against a formidable enemy, perhaps, but you need to dial that back for working.

For one thing, you're wasting all that amazing mind power on trying to get even and ruin someone else. You need to realize, in the end, it's not worth it. It will not change what happened, and all you'll achieve is making everyone else too cautious about dealing with you — so much so they'll just keep their distance. This is not particularly the best or most productive work environment to be in.

For another, you need to be mindful of becoming so lost in the constant scheming that you forget about what matters to you the most: Securing a much better position for yourself at work. At the end of the day, you need people to be able to put in a good word for you, and if all you do is cause trouble, then you might as well kiss your dreams of success goodbye.

Be mindful of your jealousy. Sometimes, things aren't what you think, despite how astute you are at judging things and people. It won't help to assume an all or nothing stance for dealing with your colleagues and bosses.

You've got to understand that humans are all different and complicated, and they won't fit neatly into the boxes you've assigned to them. They will have many motivations, relationships, friendships, and connections — and there's nothing wrong with that! Just because someone is friends with another person in a different department or company, or they're friends with someone you deeply despise, doesn't mean they could be out to get you or have betrayed you.

Learn to be at peace with the fact that you will not always be number one in the life of every member of your tribe, whether that tribe is a personal or a professional one. We all have lots of other obligations — including you! Resist the temptation to undo these other connections you don't approve of, because eventually you'll also alienate the very people you're trying to keep all to yourself. Worst-case scenario, your company will give you the boot when they learn how toxic you've been, or if you're the boss, your employees might decide there's not enough money in the world that could tempt them into staying with you.

The next time you see a colleague you value "fraternizing with the enemy," just stop, take a moment, shut your eyes, take a deep breath, exhale slowly and tell yourself it will be okay. When the people around you notice how accommodating you are, who knows? You might discover some amazing individuals you might never have known if you remained jealous.

Chapter Eight: Scorpio Sexual Compatibility

Scorpios are simply hypnotic. They brim with pure sensual and sexual magnetism. They're the one sign that has you falling in love faster than usual, with their ability to see through you, right to your very core, and that uncanny hold they have over you sexually. You may fall easy for the Scorpio, but they don't fall that easily for you — and that is by design.

The thing about being Scorpio is that it's difficult for you to trust. It's going to take a lot to get you to drop your guard and just let someone in. This is ironically part of your allure and what gives you that mysterious aura everyone is so drawn to. Nothing's sexier than the mystery you exude! People are drawn to you because they want to know what lies beneath your seemingly cool and collected exterior.

People assume that you're the type of person who's just cold, always scheming and calculating. This is far from true. You just don't want to get hurt because you feel things deeply and profoundly.

Your sexual prowess and stamina is the stuff of legends. Anyone who's been in bed with a Scorpio knows that nothing and no one else will ever compare or be as good as you. You take sex seriously; in fact, you could even say sex is sacred to you. It means surrendering to ecstasy as one, and you don't take that lightly. Also, it's how you're able to release and express the emotion you don't let out easily, which is why most Scorpios need to have lots and lots of sex.

When you're in love, you're one hundred percent committed to the other person. You're very devoted and very loyal. As far as you're concerned, this is your last stop, and you will be with them forever. Your love can border on obsession, and the more insecure you are (often because of being betrayed in the past), the more you will need to be in control, and the more you'll allow jealousy to take over you.

The Scorpio and Fidelity

You're not into being unfaithful to whoever you're with. You desire security, and so you value permanence and commitment in your relationships. The only time you ever stray was when your partner went fishing at a different lake already. You're not going to forgive or forget that without payback.

Scorpio and Aries

You both have a lot in common. You just have different styles of battle. Where Aries is quick to go in for the kill, you prefer to go for the slow burn. You'd think you both couldn't work because Aries is fire and you're water, but it's not that bad. You both have an incredibly high libido, and that can make for a lot of passion between the sheets! You'll both experience a tussle for control on account of being ruled by Mars, and you might not be willing to surrender to each other. You also will have a lot of mutual jealousy.

Scorpio and Cancer

You're well-matched with the Cancer since you're both aware of what the other person needs on a gut level. Your connection can be profound and intense. You're both very passionate, which is great because it means you'll be very intimate and loving with each other. However, the second jealousy or sexual insecurity arises, things can be blown out of proportion.

Scorpio and Libra

You're not likely to click in the beginning. The Libra keeps a cool head most of the time, and so they may not be able to relate with the Scorpio's intense passion and jealousy. Being with the Libra means you will get jealous a lot because they can be a tad indecisive when it comes to committing sexually. You love a healthy spar, but the Libra doesn't care for confrontation, and so you'll find their never-ending niceness to be disingenuous and irritating. However, once you both have a sexual relationship that is steady, you can get pretty intimate and close with each other. This is because you both value togetherness, and you put a relationship that absorbs you both above all else.

Scorpio and Capricorn

You both have a lot in common because neither of you commits to a relationship easily. You'd both rather go slow and steady. Capricorn might find your sexual passion a little too hot to handle sometimes. You, on the other hand, might think the goat a tad too distant and cold, especially in the bedroom. However, you are both very serious about love, and with some work, you can easily get through your issues.

Scorpio and Taurus

You're an amazing match! You both have a yin yang balance going on, which makes you a wonderful whole. The Taurus will need to be a bit more sensitive, and you, the Scorpio, will need to be a bit less sensitive. Also, you both need to learn to get a handle on your jealousy and sexual insecurities. However, you're both committed and loyal to one another, and you can make this work.

Scorpio and Leo

You both have high libidos. This can make things amazing in the bedroom. No one could ever accuse your love life of being dull. However, you both have a tendency to want to control the other, and you don't find it easy to give yourself fully to the other. What results is a constant battle or power struggle that can develop into full-on aggression. You're both prone to jealousy when it comes to sex, and you, in particular, Scorpio, can get very suspicious and distrustful.

Scorpio and Scorpio

Sexually, there's no denying that you're a perfect match. You're both aware of what each other wants and needs, and your souls are intertwined in an inexplicably amazing way. You're both passionate, and this means a lot of chemistry in the bedroom! The only trouble is when you both get possessive or feel sexually insecure; then issues get all out of hand. You both want to be in charge, and neither of you is interested in surrendering to the other. Your minds are ever suspicious, your egos ever vulnerable, and you can play a lot of power games when it comes to sex.

Scorpio and Aquarius

Sexually, you're both really mismatched at the start. The water bearer has a take-it-or-leave-it viewpoint and is not a fan of being tied down. This is precisely what makes you grow jealous and even resent them. For the Aquarius, you're a tad too manipulative, and they wish you would let them be rather than be so possessive. The only way things can work for you both is if you lighten up, Scorpio. Also, the water bearer must learn to be a lot more sensitive to your vulnerability and sensitivity, both of which run deep.

Scorpio and Gemini

You're both not really a match. The Gemini is quite the flirt. They can be a tad inconsistent and fickle with love. You already know without a doubt this means you will get jealous more times than you care to, and you will resent them for making you feel that way. As for the Gemini, they think you're too controlling and too possessive sexually. How to make things work between you two is simple: The Gemini needs to understand that you are a deeply passionate person, and you don't do half measures, so they need to be respectful of your feelings. On your end, Scorpio, you can try to be a little less intense. A tricky proposition, but if you set your mind to it, you can make it happen.

Scorpio and Virgo

You have a lot in common with this Earth sign. You both take your relationship seriously, and you both value security and privacy. This is great! Sure, the Virgo can find your emotional intensity a tad too overwhelming, and you might think the Scorpio way too much of an aloof, clinical prude, but because you're both willing to make a good go of your sex life, there's no problem you can't resolve together.

Scorpio and Sagittarius

This is not a perfect match by any stretch of the imagination. First, the Sagittarius has a bad case of wanderlust. They can be flirtatious with just about anyone, and this will naturally cause a Scorpio to get jealous and possessive. The only way things can work with you two is if the Sagittarius makes a conscious, continuous attempt at curbing their enthusiasm for being so flirty to respect your sensitive feelings, while you try to understand that if they love you, no matter who they flirt with, their heart is yours and yours alone.

Scorpio and Pisces

You're a great match! You're both aware instinctively of what the other is afraid of and what makes them insecure. You both connect on a very deep, incredibly tender emotional level. More than the Pisces, you'll value the physical aspect of sex. For the Pisces, what they want is more romance. They want more of your soft side. It can be a problem when you look at your Pisces as nothing more than an easy lay; you can bully into doing your bidding whenever. However, as gentle as the fish is, they're slippery, and you will have a tough time pinning them down.

Chapter Nine: The Moon Sign

Other than your Sun sign, your moon sign is just as important in astrology, as it basically affects the bits of your personality intrinsic to you. It influences the way you look at yourself. The Moon is all about feeling, instinct, and the unconscious. Contrast this to the Sun, which is all about your will. According to Evangeline Adams, where your Sun sign shows your individuality, your Moon sign shows your personality.

For astrologers, your Sun is a vital force, while your Moon is an inherent force. The Moon oversees the aspects of you, which react before you even take time to think about your reaction.

You're the only one who sees your Moon persona or instinctive behavior, which we've been socialized to keep under wraps on account of it being "uncivilized" or "brutish" or "primitive." So, your Moon persona is the part of your personality you and others would consider rather disturbing. It's the part that gives in to negative emotions and thoughts with reckless abandon. It's the part of us that we're not willing to admit exists.

The moon is also responsible for your spontaneous behavior. It's the part of you that is honest in its happiness and pleasure, and the part that always answers to emotional stimuli. It influences the part of you that wants to play in the rain, roll down a hill, pluck an apple off a tree and eat it there and then. The Moon dominates all things sensual, as in your five physical senses.

The symbolism of the Moon in astrology is a tad cryptic. It is all about your reactions and instincts from when you were a wee baby to a little child. It's a representation of your dreams, past, and memories, all of which come together to create your inner psyche.

According to astrologer Landis Knight Green, the Moon is basically an expression of your subconscious. You're in touch with your Moon sign in your daydreams and your sleeping dreams as well. It has power over your emotions, which means it governs your romantic relationships. If you're a woman with your moon in the same spot as your man's sun, you will have a well-balanced relationship. Your Moon sign is yet another reason you're different from other Scorpios.

The Scorpio Moon

Being born with your Moon in Scorpio, you're the type of person who is well in touch with the darker bits of the human psyche. You're aware of the things that are hidden from others, but this gift can be a heavy burden to bear.

As a Scorpio Moon, you're all too aware of the words left unsaid. No one does subtext better than you. No one could trick you, and as passionate as you are, you're incredibly grounded in reality.

You're secretive, and you never want to get too close to anyone, especially if you've had bad luck in love before. The anxiety you feel could be considered life and death. This is the reason you're not so keen on plunging into love with all of you.

When you're a Scorpio Moon, it can be hard for you to be as intense as the Scorpio Sun in day-to-day life. Because of this, people fear you. And because of that, you keep all your emotions locked up.

When you can't express how you feel, you're emotionally blocked, and this block will show up in your body. You get ill; often, it's a stomach-related illness since the Moon oversees the stomach.

For the Scorpio Moon, nothing less than total engagement on a soul-deep level will do in life. Yet, they always get involved in love affairs that are as passionate as they are dramatic. They need to find that same passion in other aspects of life.

You're very sensitive to everyone around you, taking on their moods, both good, bad, and neutral. You're vulnerable to dark environments where it's stagnant, heavy, toxic, and of low spiritual energy. It's important for you to find time to purge the negative emotions you feel throughout the day. With time and practice, you'll learn how to rely on your instincts with people and circumstances.

The Stillest and Deepest of Waters

When your moon is in Scorpio, you often try to seem like you've got everything under control and like it's all cool. However, a lot of brooding intensity lurk underneath that facade. You feel too deeply, and you're deathly frightened of anyone knowing that. Your friends and family know not to prove you too much.

You're secretive, and you get lost in all the emotions you feel. When you're not self-aware, you can become swallowed up by the force of emotions within you. You can get lost in revenge, jealousy, and resentment. You're a bit of a conundrum, having to repress your feelings, which only makes them way too powerful to keep locked up within. You'll learn if you haven't already that the best way to tame your inner aggression is to let the feelings out.

You're the one who totally understands everything about the human condition, and so you make an amazing criminal detective or dramatist. You would thrive in any career where your piercing insight is needed. Also, you'd be successful.

With romance and work, you must have all the avenues you can to express your many intense feelings from the depth of your emotional reservoir. Winning your trust could take years and lots of attempts to break down your walls.

Because you are a fixed sign, you don't let go of people you value easily. You hold on tight to the trusted few that have become part of your tribe. You know of how to connect with people on a deeply emotional level, and you know that you need the connections you make to feel safe and secure in your emotions.

As a Scorpio Moon, you love people willing to explore life with you deeply. You love to help them see the truth about themselves. For you, truth matters above all else. You'd rather face an ugly truth than try to dress it up so no one gets hurt because you understand that being dishonest only leads to more pain and hurt than honesty could cause in the long run.

Your sexuality is powerful. Everyone can feel it. Sometimes, desires can get very primal and make it very difficult to hold on to emotional fidelity. However, being in a relationship with you is amazing because you provide trust and sensuality in spades. You can be vengeful, moody, secretive, and resentful, but on the flip side, you're full of ambition, intense, sensual, intuitive, and imaginative.

Some folks are not happy with how you are with emotions. You might feel like no one gets you. You might detach from the circumstances you find yourself in or trying to control others, but it's only because you don't want to be hurt because you're very vulnerable. A less self-aware Scorpio will find themselves lashing out at the people around them or getting resentful and jealous. If this is you, then you need to take time out to contemplate. You need to find healthy ways to release your intense emotions. The only way you can be truly at peace is to let yourself be emotionally open.

You've got a loving heart, and you're loyal. You're in touch with other people on a psychic level. People are drawn to you; they come to you with their pain and darkest secrets. As a great friend, you offer them whatever you sense; they really need to feel better emotionally. You deal with crises better than anyone else.

Celebrities with their Moon in Scorpio

1. Thandie Newton
2. Nia Long
3. Bob Marley
4. James Dean
5. Alfred Hitchcock
6. Jason Momoa
7. Katy Perry
8. Mila Kunis
9. Eddie Murphy
10. Snoop Dog
11. Francis Ford Coppola
12. Beyonce
13. MIA
14. Alexa Chung

Chapter Ten: Scorpio Rising

The more people discuss astrology, the more they advance beyond their sun signs to understand themselves better. They look at their moon signs, check out their birth charts, and more. However, not everyone knows what a rising sign is, so we will dive into that right now.

All About Rising Signs

The Sun will typically be in each sign for 30 days, while the Moon spends only two-and-a-half days in each one. The rising sign got its name meaning, just on the horizon when you are born. You'll need to know your precise time of birth instead of an estimate to have a proper birth chart.

Where the Sun shows your deepest self, and the Moon shows your internal emotions, the ascendant or rising sign is the way you view the world, or first impression people get when they meet you. The more people get to know you, the more they see the rest of who you are. This happens over time.

Think of your rising sign as a mask you wear or a hallway with many rooms. This rising sign also defines your ruling planet, which is what fuels the energy of your sign. When astrologers consider houses, signs, and planets, they also consider the ruler of each house, sign, or planet. There's so much more to just your moon, sun, and rising sign. So, when you cannot identify with any Sun sign, remember there are other things to consider.

Finding Your Rising Sign

Again, the only way to know your rising sign is to know the precise time you were born. That means you must get your long-form birth certificate to know when that was.

When you have it, you can head on over to Astro.com, where you can get an accurate calculation of your moon, sun, and rising signs. You'll also be able to do this with apps on your phone, like TimePassages and Costar.

You need to remember that there's a lot of nuances involved in astrology. So, you might not quite agree with the description of your rising sign, but that's only because there are so many other moving parts to consider. You must think of which house your ruling planet occupies, among other factors like where the planets were relative to one another when you were born. There are so many combos and possibilities.

Scorpio Rising

As a Scorpio rising, you're alluring, quiet, and mysterious. You're charming, but it's not always sexual charm. There's always a lot going on beneath the surface, and people would love to know what gives. You're intense for good reasons. There are things you've been through that cause you to put up walls, particularly if there are other Scorpio factors influencing you, so it takes a while for you to open up enough for others to get to know you.

You have very astute and keen animal instincts. You are passionate, and you have forces within you that you can channel towards regeneration and healing, as needed by you or other people or society. Your will is strong, powerful, yet quiet and understated. You are undoubtedly a force not to be messed with. You know people's pain intuitively, and you're great at healing — or wounding, if they ever cross you. Trust your instincts, and you will achieve the greatest heights. Your ruling planets are Pluto and Mars.

Scorpio Rising and Mars in Aries: Mars is in the sign of Aries, which is courageous, motivated, and independent. You lead and blaze trails for others to follow. You're bold and original. You're a warrior, fierce in competition, possessing killer instincts which you should temper with kindness even when you mean well. Your shadow side is selfish, ruthless, and uses extreme force.

Scorpio Rising and Mars in Taurus: Mars is in Taurus, which is productive, sensual, and fertile. You're all about sensuality, satisfying your desires and appetites. You love to enjoy life like a great feast, but the best way to experience happiness is for you to not give yourself over to your cravings or overindulge. You're steady in your will, very determined, and possess the stamina you need to make your dreams happen. You're highly successful. Being obstinate and not being willing to change or let go can be problematic for you, so beware of that.

Scorpio Rising and Mars in Gemini: Mars is in Gemini, which is dexterous, clever, and skillful. You're great with your hands and possess the sharpest of reflexes. You're good with language, and it plays an important part in your destiny. Your shadow self is scheming, crafty, shrewd, and self-serving. You are gifted with words, and you can use them to heal.

Scorpio Rising and Mars in Cancer: Mars is in Cancer, which is emotional and full of soul. Your sensitivity is deep. You're very protective of animals, children, and life in general. You are naturally empathic and can connect with your surroundings on an emotional level. You're passionate, and you're very sensuous. You won't find it easy to communicate, understand, or articulate your feelings so it makes sense intellectually or rationally. You find it easiest to communicate using music.

Scorpio Rising and Mars in Leo: Mars is in the confident, proud, and ever radiant Leo. You have a lot of willpower, and you would make a great leader, able to influence people by the thousands because of your magnetism. You have a strong, intense, vital force, which along with your consistent focus, helps you to carry out your noble ideals. You must make use of your personal power the right way. Your shadow self can be tyrannical.

Scorpio Rising and Mars in Virgo: Mars in Virgo means you're about special skills, service, technical know-how, and knowledge in general. You're interested in health sciences, medicine, chemistry, and biology. You are very astute in your observations, and you analyze things well. Your work is ever efficient and thorough, mostly because of your obsession. When you're not balanced, you get overly worried and critical of yourself and the world. You're usually the force behind a king or acting as a shrewd advisor.

Scorpio Rising and Mars in Libra: You have a desire to cooperate with others. You love to work in reams, and you always find a way to balance everyone's needs, including your own. Your actions are because of your need for connection, beauty, and harmony. You need to be wary of suppressing your desires and not acting for your own sake, as this can lead to conflict and hidden anger. Remain honest in all you do, and whatever you do, and don't try to make your goals happen secretly or by using others. Bring them together and choose to always be fair.

Scorpio Rising and Mars in Scorpio: You're at one with nature's primal forces. You need to remain connected to nature in an uncivilized, raw, and wild way. You give off the energies of death and birth, destructiveness, and creativeness, and you get why both ends of the spectrum are essential. Your physical presence is palpable, and you're full of passion and vitality, which you could use for good or bad. Learn your power and learn what it means to have it and use it. It can be your strength, and it can heal you and others. For you, what matters more is how intense experience is, and not its permanence.

Scorpio Rising and Mars in Sagittarius: You're adventurous, expansive, and spirited. You're all about the future. You're drawn to risk, and you love challenges. The more dangerous the pursuit, the better. You're very philosophical and idealistic, using your convictions and need for fairness to check your instincts. You're all about passion and zeal. When you're not balanced, you get self-righteous, zealous, and reckless. When you're at your best, you love to explore, and you inspire others. For you, there is much joy in adventure and exploring life.

Scorpio Rising and Mars in Capricorn: You're ambitious, practical, and earthy. You love goals that are tangible and material accomplishments. You get the way the world works, and you always calculate before you get going on making your goal happen. You have a great work ethic, self-discipline, and self-sacrifice. You can become a workaholic. For you, your ambition in terms of career is more important than anything else. You can also be in a place of authority if you desire.

Scorpio Rising and Mars in Aquarius: You're about the collective. You're unconventional and a free thinker. You are interested in regenerating society as we know it. You know of the problems plaguing mankind, and you know how to create solutions that are most innovative, either on your own or with others. You're at your best playing a group leader, a dissident, or a reformer.

Scorpio Rising and Mars in Pisces: Visionary, dreamy, and imaginative describe you. You're open spiritually, which means you can easily connect with other realms or enter altered states of consciousness. You use art or visualization to heal yourself and others. You're not great with intoxicants like alcohol, as they make you feel powerless and confused. You have amazing psychic abilities, which can become even more pronounced if you want them to be.

Scorpio Rising and Pluto in Aries: You've got a passion for being a hero and a person all on your own. You're free. You're a daredevil. You're bold, and you've got arrogant confidence, which could be your undoing if you're not careful.

Scorpio Rising and Pluto in Taurus: You're stubborn, willful, inflexible. You are obsessed with economics, wealth, and money. This could dictate your destiny.

Scorpio Rising and Pluto in Gemini: You need to understand everyone and everything. You value education and intellect. You're driven to use your head.

Scorpio Rising and Pluto in Cancer: You need to let go of all old conditioning and the familiar ruts you're in. You need to let go of all the loads the old world has placed upon your shoulders so you can regenerate and use your powers for good.

Scorpio Rising and Pluto in Leo: You've got to let go of your desire to fawn over those who are charismatic. You need to stop loving power so much. You get into self-glorification, use a lot of self-will, and pay attention to just you and your desires. You need to deal with this if you are to attain your greatest ideals.

Scorpio Rising and Pluto in Virgo: You desire perfection. You feel you must purify yourself, and this need can become a tad obsessive. You feel guilt over a lot of things, whether the wrongs are real or in your head. You are great at perfection, technical expertise, and analyzing everything in-depth. Your work is ever so precise.

Scorpio Rising and Pluto in Libra: You crave equality, justice, and fairness. You want to balance. You see corruption and injustice, and you desire to bring this to light so it can end. You're also concerned about how the balance of power plays out in your personal relationships.

Scorpio Rising and Pluto in Scorpio: You can go to the darkest depths just to give the world some light, consciousness, and healing. When you use your powers for selfish gain, you feel like you're all alone, and you become your worst adversary. You know of rapture, depth, and things that are horrific. You could be the best of healers, perhaps even a Shaman, if your heart is in the right place.

Scorpio Rising and Pluto in Sagittarius: You need to revise, to cleanse, and to take your beliefs about how life works even further. You need to get rid of your inherent dogmatism and overzealousness, and your biased convictions, so you can attain the highest of heights.

Scorpio Rising and Pluto in Capricorn: You can breakdown and buildup society, from businesses all the way to the government. You need to get rid of hypocrisy, corruption, and greed, and there is no one better suited to this work than you are. You have a very strong will, and you need to tamp that down with kindness and humility.

Conclusion

Dear Scorpio, you're amazing! Know that. You're the one sign in the zodiac that is often misunderstood, so my sincerest hope is that I've been able to help you and others understand what you're really like. No one could possibly match the intensity of feelings in your heart, and this is a great thing when you're at your most loving, willing to allow yourself to be vulnerable and open.

Love everything about who you are and never have to apologize for it. This is not a pass for you to be a crappy person when you're at your worst. I simply mean that when you do feel low, you need to remember your best qualities and aspire to "strengthen your strengths," so to speak.

Learn to be more trusting of people. The fact is that people can and will continue to disappoint. After all, we're humans, and there's no such thing as the perfect Sun sign, Moon sign, house, or decan or what have you. So be willing to trust because the more you trust, the better your intuition gets at discovering who's right for your tribe and who isn't.

We've finally come to the end of this book, and with any luck, you now have a deeper, clearer understanding of who you really are. There's nothing wrong with you, dearest Scorpio! You're amazing, so own it!

Here's another book by Mari Silva that you might like

References

12 Astrology Zodiac Signs Dates, Meanings and Compatibility. (n.d.). Www.Astrology-Zodiac-Signs.Com. https://www.astrology-zodiac-signs.com/

Astrology - All Sun Moon Combinations. (n.d.). Astrology-Numerology.Com. from http://astrology-numerology.com/sun-moon.html

Astrology King. (n.d.). Astrology King. http://astrologyking.com

Astrology Library. (n.d.). Astrolibrary.Org. https://astrolibrary.org/

Birth Chart Interpretations -Planets in Signs and Houses. (n.d.). Astrolibrary.Org. https://astrolibrary.org/interpretations/

Horoscope and Astrology - Homepage. (2019). Astro.Com. http://astro.com

Personality & Relationship Astrology: Compatibility, Attraction and Sign Personality Traits. (n.d.). South Florida Astrologer - Personality & Relationship Astrology. https://www.southfloridaastrologer.com/

The Best Online Astrology Resources. (n.d.). ♄. https://bangtanastrology.tumblr.com/post/169791137127/the-best-online-astrology-resources

www.ingramcontent.com/pod-product-compliance
Lightning Source LLC
Chambersburg PA
CBHW050512240426
4367JCB00004B/196